Too Much
Is Not Enough

Also by Orson Bean
Me and the Orgone

Too Much Is Not Enough

by Orson Bean

Lyle Stuart Inc.   *Secaucus, New Jersey*

Published by Lyle Stuart, Inc.
120 Enterprise Ave., Secaucus, N.J. 07094
In Canada: Musson Book Company
a division of General Publishing Co. Limited
Don Mills, Ontario

Manufactured in the United States of America

Library of Congress Cataloging-in-Publication Data

Bean, Orson.
    Too much is not enough.

    1. Bean Orson. 2. Television actors and actresses--
United States--Biography. I. Title.
PN2287.B3937A3   1988   791.45'028'0924   [B]   88-2116
ISBN 0-8184-0465-5

This book is dedicated
with deep gratitude
to the memory of
Bill W.

I want to thank David Blasband, Sam
Bobrick, Professor Richard Brown, John
Robben and Herb Goldberg for their
encouragement and assistance, and Howard
Ostroff for his invaluable help with the
structure of this book. In Herb Goldberg's
book *The New Male-Female Relationship*
(Signet) you'll find an expansion of the
ideas attributed to him in the last chapter.
I recommend it.

Take what you want,
Said God,
And pay for it.

—OLD SPANISH PROVERB

Foreword

Early on in the game I decided that it would not satisfy me to be less than the happiest son of a bitch who ever lived. I prided myself on being clever enough, inventive enough, courageous enough, whatever it took enough to be able to have those people and things in my life necessary for happiness. My ego was in great shape. I chewed up careers and spit them out. I went through money like I'd invented it and kept on earning more. I married two fine women and raised four wonderful kids. I traveled the world, wrote books, produced plays, founded and administrated a school for children, starred on Broadway for years at a crack, hosted *The Tonight Show* a hundred times, designed and built houses, made movies and spun my way across the Board Game of Life.

In 1980, when I was 52, the joy ride came to an abrupt halt. My second marriage of fourteen years ended in a painful divorce, my show business career dried up and I began to question my ability to function as a human being. I fell into deep despair and became a virtual recluse. For three years I ventured out of my bachelor apartment in New York only to work or spend time with my children. My life had hit the bottom of the barrel.

One day, while sitting alone in my kitchen, I heard the sound of laughter. I looked around and nobody was there. I realized then that I was the laugher and that I was cackling for pure joy. "Hold everything," I muttered. "I've got no reason to be happy."

Then it hit me. I didn't need a reason. I had simply become bored with being unhappy. The consequences of this realization were staggering to me. (They shouldn't have been, because I'd been learning variations on the theme my whole life.) Being unhappy was something I'd been *doing*; when I stopped doing it, I reverted to my natural state, which is happiness. Everything I'd felt I needed in my life in order to be happy—family, career, celebrity status, money—was gone, and here I was feeling blissful. I danced for joy on the linoleum floor.

The feeling, of course, did not last. In short order, the usual litany of complaints took their place in my head and I reverted to depression. I was determined to find out what was going on. Why in the name of God would I choose to be unhappy when I knew I could be happy? In time the answer came to me. Control. I wanted to feel in control. Being happy without apparent cause made me nervous. I wasn't "doing" it. My ego seemed to insist on being in charge, even when there was nothing in it for me. I thought I wanted to be happy, but my ego insisted on my being miserable.

"Wait a minute," I thought. "Maybe I'm on to something. It's almost as if my ego is a separate thing from me. Who the hell am I, anyway?" I'd always identified myself with my ego. But in my years as an actor, I'd had ample opportunity to learn that my ego is frequently the enemy. Its specialties are stage fright and shallowness.

So if I'm not my ego, who am I? I was determined to ferret out a logical answer to that question. The mind/body/personality known as Orson, I reasoned, is sort of an organization made up of millions upon millions of brain cells, heart cells, blood cells, skin cells, etc., which cluster

together to make up portions and ultimately the whole of
Orson. These function in more or less autonomous
fashion. I don't make my heart beat or my lungs breathe
or my eyes see. I don't make my mind function, either.
Stuff keeps popping into it from God knows where. The
problem, if anything, is not making it function but keeping it still.

If I had a frontal lobotomy, my body would still continue to function. Conversely, were I to become completely paralyzed, my mind would keep on working. In
neither case would I *do* anything to make any of this happen . . . and the "I" that wouldn't do anything is my ego.
So where did I get the idea that my ego is so damned
important? The ego in the Orson organization is in fact a
minor civil servant, a flunky, a functionary to help collect
thoughts and perceptions to be catalogued and stored in
the brain. I (whoever that is) need an ego just as I need a
liver. But to say that either of them is "me" or "in charge"
is bananas.

My ego is on an ego trip, I decided. So I voted to give it
a gold watch and retire it as chairman of the board. My
poor ego, like Marcos and Duvalier, screamed blue
murder for a long time. But in the end it too was a straw
man.

So, who's in charge of me, anyway? As far as I can see,
the answer is no one. The Orson group is a physical, men-
tal and emotional democracy. To the extent that I trust
things to work out, they appear to do so. For instance,
when I don't worry about my health, I feel fine. When
I'm not concerned about money, I always seem to have
enough. When I'm not trying to be attractive to the opposite sex, women are drawn to me. When I'm not trying to
impress the audience or critics, my acting is wonderful.
There really seems to be some kind of process that takes
over when "I" let go of control. But what the hell is it?

The awful thought pops into my head: "Oh, God . . .
It's God." Oh no. Not that. I'm not going on a religious
trip. Religious people are wimps. Christians with their
polyester suits; California veggies with their carrots.

Aargh! Shudder. Not God. Don't tell me it's come to that! But who or what else runs things so well when *I* stop trying to run them?

Alright, Bean. Don't panic. One step at a time. Religion. Hmm. I sure can't swallow the traditional Christian stuff. The dogma is such a turnoff. The dogma of all religions is a turnoff: contradictory, judgmental and arbitrary. (Jesus would have hated it.) Well, not to worry about the dogma. I can pick and choose what I want from a smorgasbord of religions . . . or I can forget about all of it. As dogma goes, reincarnation makes sense to me. Always has. Much more than the Christian "once around" theory. I mean, if you only have one shot and you spend it as the Elephant Man, life is a cruel joke. Of course, the reincarnation crowd is as bonkers as the rest. How come they all remember their past life as an Egyptian princess? Wasn't anyone ever incarnated as a plumber in Cleveland?

I need to understand what's going on. That's why I sat down and started writing about my life. Not for you to read, although that's nice, too. For *me*. Do you think I'm crazy? You bought the book.

Venice, California, 1987

I

Looking back, I realize that a certain amount of confusion was inevitable. People who are born on the 22nd of the month never know which sign to go by in the Daily Horoscope. Not that I give much credence to any of that stuff, but still . . .

There's a joke about a guy who is killing time in Grand Central Station. He drops a coin into a public scale and a ticket comes out which reads: "You weigh 175 pounds, you are a Jew and you are catching the 5:15 to Larchmont." The guy can't believe his eyes. He steps off the scale, watches other people get different fortunes from it and then tries again. Once more, his card says: "You weigh 175 pounds, you are a Jew and you are catching the 5:15 to Larchmont." The guy freaks. He paces the floor in agitation. In front of the gate for the train to Buffalo, he spots an Indian in a feathered headdress.

"I'll give you twenty bucks if you'll come into the men's room and switch clothes with me," he says to the Indian. "You can have your stuff back in a few minutes." The

Indian agrees, the man changes wardrobe and returns to the infamous scale. This time his card reads: "You still weigh 175 pounds, you are still a Jew and while you were fucking around with that Indian in the men's room, you missed the 5:15 to Larchmont."

Life offers what it will, and thinking about it too much is not helpful. A group of Talmudic scholars once asked the question: Should man have been created or was he a mistake? After years of debate, they finally decided on their answer: No. Man should not have been created, but since he has been, he might as well make the best of it.

My childhood, like most people's, was pretty dreadful, but I only realized that later. At the time, having nothing to compare it to, I thought I was doing fine. I was born on July 22nd (Atilla the Hun's birthday), 1928, in Burlington, Vermont, under the name of Dallas Burrows, a handle which I subsequently discarded. My mother, an auburn-haired New England beauty, was of staunch Republican stock. Her grandmother and Calvin Coolidge's mother were sisters and Mom lived in the White House for a while when "Cousin Cal" was president. Her ancestors went back to the Revolution and General Putnam, an early American war hero.

My father was a New Deal Democrat from Boston, his parents immigrants who met after coming to this country, she from Scotland, he from Ireland. They had several children, all of whom except my father died early, one in a fiery car crash. One day, Grandpa Burrows went to the grocery store for a pound of butter and never came back.

If I ever met any of my father's family, I don't remember them, but I knew and loved my mother's people, especially her father. His name was Dallas Pollard. He'd been called that after James Polk's vice president. Why anyone would name their kid after an obscure president's even more obscure vice president I don't know, but my grandfather's parents did and mine named me after him. So I suffered from the name Dallas; as soon as I grew up and moved out, I changed it.

My granddad was nuts about his daughter, so it must have pained the old man dearly when she married my father. I don't know what the nature of her rebellion was, but the stalwart Vermont conservative found himself with a son-in-law who believed in the New Deal before Roosevelt thought it up. A law student he was, and my mother with her brown eyes and beautiful breasts must have driven him crazy. I know she did me.

Grandpa was a wonderful and funny man. A Vermonter through and through, he was an insular soul who used to warn me against southerners. "Stay away from Hartford," he'd say. He was married to my grandmother for sixty years. When she died, he got married again at the age of eighty-five to a lady of eighty-five, whom he used to go with before he married my grandmother.

I did my early childhood years in Cambridge, Massachusetts, where I lived in the bottom half of a two-family house with my immediate antecedents and no brothers and sisters. My life was full of politics. Once when I was little, a poor Black guy came to our place to a fund raising affair, one of endless such affairs which my mother and father gave for various left wing causes. Prompted by my folks to do so, I trotted out my autograph book and asked him to sign it. He wrote, in a childish scrawl, "Olin Montgomery, one of the Scottsboro Boys." I can still remember his frightened eyes as he looked around our living room at the various liberals, Fellow Travelers and Parlor Pinks who stood there with cocktails in their hands. The Scottsboro Boys were a group of Black youths who had been unjustly accused of raping a white girl in the town of Scottsboro, Georgia. The Party had championed their cause and somehow gotten them out of jail. Then, having nothing better to do with them, they shipped them around to fund raisers, where innocent do-gooders like my mother and father sold glasses of rye and ginger at 50¢ a shot, "for the cause."

All it meant to me was a chance to rifle a few of the purses that were thrown with the guests' coats onto my bed. Even though I was one of "the people," nobody ever asked me whether it was alright to use my room to check coats in, so I simply looked at the thievery as tip money.

When I was eight years old, my folks gave me a Gilbert Magic Set and I went crazy for it: cups and balls, Chinese sticks, linking rings, the works. I carried the box to my room, lovingly examined each piece of apparatus, studied the instructions and vowed on the spot that some day I'd become a professional magician. As the years went by, my ambition never wavered. While other boys dreamed of being firemen or agents of the FBI, I pictured myself levitating ladies on the stage of the RKO Boston Theater.

My mother's and father's marriage was, to say the least, tempestuous. She began to threaten suicide when I was about six. "If your father ever leaves me, I'll kill myself," she said. "If you want me to stay alive, it's your job to keep him around." I accepted the responsibility. My parents would have an argument and he'd storm out of the house.

"Take me with you," I'd cry, running after him. I wanted to make sure he wouldn't be leaving for good.

"When you come back, you'll find me dead on the kitchen floor in front of the gas stove," my mother would scream from the window as we headed up the street.

"Come on, Dallas," my father would say. I'd take his hand and walk away with him, glancing back toward the house to see my mother's stricken face at the window.

We'd wander the neighborhood for an hour, on what my father called a meander. He genuinely loved me. He'd talk to me about politics and the war. In my mind, I'd picture the kitchen floor, wondering if she was lying on it in front of the open gas stove.

"Do you think we ought to go back now? Maybe she really did it this time."

"She'll never really do it, believe me." But after a while, we would go back. As we'd round the corner of our block, the curtain at our front window would always be fluttering slightly.

"See there." My father would point to the window. "That's where she's been standing, watching for us. You don't have to worry, I tell you."

We'd walk into the house and be hit by the smell of gas. "Come on," my father would say. "We'll wait in the bedroom." Into my mother's and father's room we'd go, and shut the door and open the windows and wait.

"Ha, ha. Oh boy, what a charade."

"That gas smell is pretty strong, George." I called him George; we were a modern family, with books that said that parents and their children should be friends. "Do you think we just ought to go and see?"

"You've got to trust me. She's fine. She'll be out any minute now."

And sure enough out she'd come, after a while. Haggard, furious that her bluff had been called, she'd stand at the bedroom door, her eyes filled with hatred and mortification.

"Damn you," she'd spit at him. I'd assume his mocking smile. I wanted to run to her and hold her and cry, "I brought him back, don't you see?" I knew that an hour later, they'd be locked in their bedroom making love. My father was the center and purpose of my mother's life. I'd been sent from Central Casting to play the small but dramatic role of the son.

"Some day I'll grow up and get out of here." I told myself. "I'll keep her alive as long as I can and then I'll make my break."

I went to public school in Cambridge, despising every minute of it. I felt that the only way I could survive was to drive the teachers crazier than I believed they were trying to drive me. (There were exceptions, of course, like dear old Mr. Bartlett.) As a result, I spent a great deal of time in the dean's office.

Years later, when I was in my forties, I got a job shooting an industrial film at a small shoe factory in Kansas. While the technicians were setting up the lights, I wandered into the company cafeteria to have a cup of coffee.

It was a little after ten in the morning. Precisely at 10:10 a bell rang. Almost immediately the doors of the cafeteria flew open and a flood of forty or so factory workers rushed in. Thirstily, they headed for the coffee machines, then moved to the room's long tables, laughing and gossiping, carrying their polyurethane cups of steaming java.

Exactly fifteen minutes later, at 10:25, a second bell rang. The workers got up, deposited their empty cups in the plastic bins by the doors and moved back to their machines.

Sitting there in the corner of the cafeteria, it suddenly dawned on me what school had been all about. It was the bells. What they had taught in between the bells was irrelevant: isosceles triangles, Hannibal crossing the Alps, i before e; they were all interchangeable. What they had spent years drumming into our heads was this: a bell rings, it's time to be interested in math. The next bell rings, it's time to stop being interested in math and start being interested in history. Next bell: put history out of your mind and become interested in English.

A kid who wants to work on math all day is a troublemaker. A worker who wants coffee at 9:45 is a disruptive influence. Preparation For Life I: Listen to the bells. Being a troublemaker, I didn't.

Every Thursday at noon during the war years a new vaudeville show would open at the RKO Boston, a movie palace of the grand old style. When it did so, 70 percent of the audience would consist of boys playing hooky from high schools in the greater Boston area. Down the aisles of the theater would prowl truant officers, shining their flashlights across row after row of the young patrons, hoping to spot a familiar face. As the beam of light drew close, adolescent heads (mine among them) would pop down out of sight, then pop up again after the bounty hunter had passed.

An actor/magician named John Calvert brought his show to Boston. Calvert was one of several Hollywood leading men who starred as The Falcon in a series of B mystery movies. The RKO ran big ads in *The Globe* when Calvert's magic show came to town. SEE! ... COLD BLOODED MURDER COMMITTED ON STAGE AT EVERY PERFORMANCE!

Calvert appeared as a mad scientist in a laboratory. His assistants were bountifully endowed young women in nurses' uniforms. In the middle of a lab was a table with a buzzsaw attached to it. One of the nurses would hand Calvert a beaker of foaming, bubbling liquid to drink.

"Dry ice in water," I'd explain to the kid next to me. I knew how these effects were created. Calvert quaffed the potient, then let out a terrible scream and bent over, clutching his stomach. Up in the light booth, the electrician slid a green gel in front of the spot. Calvert slipped a pair of hideous false teeth into his mouth, then slowly straightened and glowered at the audience. The effect was electrifying. Suddenly, without warning, he made a great leap from the stage, cleared the orchestra pit and landed in the center aisle of the audience. Pandemonium broke out. A planted stooge jumped out of his seat and ran from the theater.

Calvert, followed by the green spot, clambered ape-like through the crowd. Then he seized a young woman, seemingly a member of the audience, and dragged her screaming onto the stage. Quickly the nurses strapped her onto the dissecting table and the buzzsaw was turned on. With tremendous showmanship, Calvert had turned a run-of-the-mill Sawing a Woman in Half illusion into a theatrical event.

Calvert the magician was my hero. In my bedroom at home I spent hours each day practicing sleight of hand in front of the mirror on my bureau and as time went by I developed an act I could perform at church suppers to earn spending money.

In 1944 I was 16 and my father had had enough. I guess he figured I was old enough to look after myself, and he was right. He announced that he had quit his job at the defense plant where he'd been working and had accepted a position with the government on the island of Adak, in the Aleutian chain off Alaska. It would be a chance, he said, for him to make some real money. A few days later he left, amidst great sturm and drang, and my mother began spending most of her time in neighborhood bars.

I decided to move out then too. I had an after-school job as a bus boy at a local restaurant. With so many men off at war, there were lots of jobs available to industrious kids. I took a furnished room a few blocks from our house and bought a radio. A great weight lifted from me. Now that my father was gone, there was no longer anything I could do to keep my mother alive . . . and when there's nothing you can do, you don't have to do anything.

A week after I'd left, my mother called me on the phone at the restaurant where I worked.

"Please come see me," she pleaded.

"No," I answered. I loved her more than anything in the world. All my life I had ached for her approval, longed for a glimpse of that look in her eyes which would mean to a little boy, "You're wonderful, special, unique." I had never seen it. For longer than I could remember, I had let her manipulate me into convincing my father to stay with her. Now he was gone and I knew she was going to kill herself. And because I loved her, I wanted her to get the dying over with. But I wouldn't stay around to watch. Enough pain was enough. "I'm not coming to see you," I told her and hung up the phone.

The following morning I was in my home room at school when the door opened and a kid walked in. He handed the teacher a note, then whispered to her. She looked up and found me with her eyes. I knew what the note said. It didn't matter. Nothing mattered. Crazily, I felt like laughing.

"Mr. Burke wants to see you, Dallas."

My footsteps echoed on the dark, oiled floors of the corridor as I trod the familiar path to the dean's office. I felt lighter than air. What the hell. I didn't need her. I didn't need anyone. I knocked on the receptionist's door and walked in. She didn't meet my eyes. "You may go right in, Dallas." I opened the door to the inner office. My aunt was standing next to Mr. Burke. She lived in Winchester, where she raised two small children alone. Her husband, my mother's younger brother, was a medical officer with the Navy, on duty in the South Pacific. Neither she nor the dean looked at me as I came in.

"Well, Dallas," said my aunt when we were outside on the wide granite steps of the ancient school building, "your mother is dead."

All you boys whose mothers are still living take one step forward. Not so fast, Burrows.

"How did she . . . how did it happen?"

My aunt turned away. Does she think it's my fault, I wondered?

"She just . . . apparently . . . stuck her head in the oven and turned on the gas."

I glanced at the school behind me. A kid I didn't recognize was looking out the window. "I wonder if he knows about me?" I thought. "Knows that I'm unlovable."

We got into my aunt's car and drove to the house I had shared with my mother and father. The back door was unlocked. The police had taken away my mother's body and there was no one there. The door to the oven was open and any army blanket lay on the linoleum-covered floor in front of it.

I folded the army blanket and put it in the closet. I closed the oven door and straightened up the kitchen. I walked over to the First National Store and asked for some empty boxes. Then I went home and began packing our stuff for storage. Eight months later, my father came back from Adak and we moved into an apartment in Harvard Square. We never talked about what had happened.

In June of 1946 I graduated from high school ("Free, great God, free at last!"). I had decided to enlist in the Army. Since I had no interest in going on to college it seemed like the logical thing to do. The war was over and America was occupying Germany and Japan. Duty to

God and country could be gotten out of the way in eighteen months back then. It was a good deal and a lot of boys who didn't take advantage of it found themselves serving long, miserable hitches in Korea a few years later.

I joined the service with my high school buddy Parker Swann. We'd been boy magicians together and were inseparable. Or so we thought. On our second day in the army, at Fort Dix, New Jersey, a placement center, I committed a minor infraction of some kind and was sent off to "clean the grease traps" in the kitchen. When I returned from my eight-hour ordeal, the barracks where Parker and I had slept the night before was empty. There was no sign of where my group had been shipped to. My newly issued duffle bag was gone too, with all my clothes, army and civilian, and the induction papers which proved who I was. There was nothing left in the building but forty iron cots with rolled-up mattresses on them.

I rushed outside and hailed a passing non-com.

"Somebody has stolen all my stuff," I whimpered. He gazed at my pale kid's face under its newly chopped-off G.I. haircut.

"Steal somebody else's," he said, and walked on. I went back into the barracks and unfolded a mattress onto one of the iron cots. Then I placed another mattress on top of it and crawled between them. Eventually, I fell asleep, feeling lonelier than I ever had in my life.

In the morning I somehow wrangled a new issue of equipment and when the next batch of enlistees arrived, I joined them and shipped out to Fort Knox, Kentucky, where I underwent two months of basic training. Then I traveled by troop train (oy!) across the country to the port of San Francisco for assignment overseas. (My original group, I discovered later, had been sent to Texas, where the Army taught Parker Swann how to be a cook.)

In December of 1946, after a night on the town in San Francisco, where I became a man at "McGee's Hotel—Where You Can Always Get In," I sailed for Yokohama on a "Victory Boat," a cargo scow refurbished by the U.S. government for purposes of troop transport. As the ship pulled out of San Francisco bay, I began to feel seasick. The G.I.s slept in hammocks stacked four deep. Mine was second from the bottom. The trip took eight days, along the coast of Alaska and the Aleutian Islands. The compartment I slept in was next to the mess. They served oranges. For years afterwards, the smell of oranges nauseated me.

The ship rose up on heavy North Pacific seas, then slammed back down again. On December 24th, in the night, we crossed the International Date Line, then woke up on December 26th. That's the kind of trip it was. The Red Cross gave each of us a box containing a toothbrush, a bar of soap and a cookie. Almost all of the new, young soldiers on board the ship were desperately seasick; a handful weren't. These lucky individuals strolled past my hammock on their way to the mess, where they ate their food as well as mine. As they went by, they whistled cheerfully. I hated them, and as my misery grew, so did my hatred. Ultimately, I wanted to kill them, just because they weren't sick. It was a bad feeling and I've never forgotten it.

In Yokohama we froze our cojones off in tents. Then I found myself assigned to the 81st Airborne Artillery outside the little town of Koi Zumi, 50 miles north of Tokyo. I spent a year there, living in a converted aircraft factory, learning to handle howitzers and pulling guard duty. In the nearby village, Japanese women still walked around bare breasted; men relieved themselves against walls; occasional smoke-belching buses chugged past, powered by wood burning stoves strapped to their back bumpers. American cigarettes were the local unit of exchange.

On days off, I'd catch the train to Tokyo. As the train approached the city, all was desolation; there was nothing left standing but smoke stacks. General Doolittle had firebombed Tokyo around the clock for weeks on end. The physical destruction was as great as Hiroshima's. Constructed around the bottoms of the smoke stacks were little huts made of scrap wood or corrugated tin. A whisp of smoke rose from each tall chimney, showing that the family that lived in the shack below was cooking its meager dinner.

We read in *Stars and Stripes* that occupation troops in Germany were being murdered every day, picked off by unreconstructed Nazi snipers. In Tokyo, we could stroll the darkest alley at midnight with no fear. The Emperor had told his people to accept MacArthur as their leader and they had done so.

I wrangled a job managing the base movie theater. Whenever I could, I put on magic shows for the troops. Extracurricular activities like this cut down on guard duty and kept me away from the grease traps. By now I was quite an accomplished magician. The climax of my act came when I'd call four or five soldiers out of the audience and hypnotize them. Then I'd have them fall down, get stuck to the floor, become attached to one another and in general make fools of themselves. The audience of G.I.s would go crazy.

The act was a complete fake. My secret consisted of whispering into the ears of my volunteers that they should do whatever I said. To my habitual astonishment, they always did so. People, it seems, are terrified when they're on stage in front of a crowd, and are only too happy to be told what to do. By the time the performance was over and they'd been given an ovation by the audience, they were heroes. When they returned to their seats, their friends would cluster around them.

"Were you really hypnotized?" they'd be asked. If they said yes they remained objects of awe and admiration, celebrities for the night. If they'd answered, "No, he whispered in my ear," they'd have been regarded as idiots. They always kept my secret.

When my hitch in the Army was done, I returned to Boston and moved into a shabby theatrical rooming house called The Carlton. Comics, magicians, dance teams and ventriloquists stayed there while they were playing the Boston area. I was determined to break into show business. It was 1948. Radio was on the way out; television hadn't yet come into its own. Live entertainment was thriving. There was a full year's work in the New England area. Split weeks and full weeks. Manufacturing towns like Lowell, Lawrence and Fall River, Massachusetts; or Pawtucket, Rhode Island, boasted blue collar clubs with names like The Latin Quarter or The Trocadero. The pay for most entertainers in these spots was $75 for a six-day week or $15 a night for weekend bookings; not bad when you consider that a hamburger at The White Tower cost a nickle.

I began to get work as a comedy magician and master of ceremonies. The M.C. in a night club had to do "time." In other words, if the show was supposed to last an hour and the other acts could only do twelve minutes each, he stretched his performance. In most of the clubs, business was sparse during the week and big on Saturdays. On that night, long tables of twenty to thirty people (bowling leagues, etc.) would ring the dance floor like spokes of a wheel. The comic would hope for a fat lady with an infectious laugh to be in the audience. If he found one, he'd play to her.

In out-of-town dates, one entertainer who owned a car would have to be booked on the bill. He would collect $1.50 a night from each of the other acts who rode with him. Once I was engaged for the weekend at a place called The Melody Lounge in Pawtucket. Opening night was December 24th. As showtime approached, there was not a single customer in the club. The performers were nervously waiting backstage (the kitchen). As M.C., I approached the boss, a heavyset Portuguese guy. "Do we have to go on?" I asked.

"I pay. You make the show," he answered sourly. He stood next to the silent cash register at the end of the bar. I smiled at the bartender, hoping he'd return the favor when I was out on the dance floor.

Just as the show was about to start, a couple walked in and sat at a side table. They were having an argument. The three-piece band (piano, drums and sax) played an overture ("There's No Business Like Show Business") and I came out onto the floor and strode to the microphone.

"Good evening ladies and germs," I said. "It's showtime here at The Melody Lounge and I wanna tell you, business is so bad I'm going snow blind from the tablecloths." The muted sounds of the couple's argument drifted through the room.

What the hell am I going to do when it's time for the audience participation part of my act, I wondered? I introduced the dance team and they went on. The couple in the audience never looked up. It's Christmas Eve, I thought, who in hell would want to spend it in a cheap nightclub? My girlfriend Ruthie would. She had come along to be with me for the evening. I was crazy about her. I'd ordered her a hot turkey sandwich and a 7-Up and she sat in the back of the club at a table near the bar, eating the sandwich and watching me sweat.

As it came time for me to do my act, I saw the wife from the quarreling couple get up and go to the ladies' room. I opened my spot by making a bird cage with a rubber canary in it disappear. Then I did a floating handkerchief trick. Neither appealed to the guy, who sat staring into his rum and Coke. I rolled some sheets of newspapers into a tube, tore it a couple of times and then pulled out a tall paper tree. The three-piece band played a chord. From the back of the house, Ruthie applauded. The boss glared at her and she stopped clapping.

Now I had to get someone out onto the floor and hypnotize him, or there was no way I could do enough time to fill the show. The guy's wife was still in the ladies' room. In desperation, I asked him if he'd be my assistant. To my absolute astonishment, he agreed. There was now no audience at all left to watch the show. I whispered in the guy's ear that he should do what I told him. Who was I trying to keep it a secret from? The guy did whatever I wanted. He fell down on the floor, got stuck on it and clucked like a chicken. At some point, his wife came out of the ladies' room and, upon seeing her husband on stage, turned her chair around and faced the back of the club.

I finished my act and asked for a big hand for my assistant. There was no one to applaud. I asked for a big hand for the band. My eyes were glassy and I was operating by rote. I wondered whether the Portuguese guy was going to make us do a second show. I went back to my dressing room (a nail). The guy from the dance team asked how the show had gone. "Wonderful," I said. I changed my clothes and went out into the club. My assistant and his wife had gone home. The owner called me over to his cash register. "You stink," he said, and handed me fifteen dollars.

"You don't want me back for Saturday and Sunday?" I asked. He made a little barking noise that I took to mean no.

We did not have to do a second show. I'd been "cancelled" on Christmas Eve and had fifteen dollars. The male half of the dance team drove the car, which then took us back to Boston. He charged me an extra $1.50 for Ruthie's ride, explaining that he was sorry to have to do so. I'd had to pay for her hot turkey sandwich, and would have to lay out 10 percent of my salary to the agent who booked the club, and 5 percent (75¢) to a so-called personal manager I employed, by the name of Fred Mack, who made phone calls to agents and read lists of performers to them, helping them to book the shows. This left me with $8.25 to live on for the week (for all I knew, for the rest of my life). My rent at the Carlton was $11. I figured things would work out. I don't remember how, but they did.

I wasn't always booked on shows as the M.C. Because I did magic, sometimes I was booked as the novelty act with another comic. This allowed me to steal jokes from my partners and memorize them for future use. I was more interested in being a comic than I was in being a magician. A comedian named Billy Garrigan was the permanent M.C. at a club in Revere Beach called Murphy's By The Sea. To the tune of "Pistol Packin' Mama," he improvised verses I still remember: "Bali Bali, isle of sin.

Girls wear nothin' but a great big grin. There's two guys they won't let in. Charlie Chaplin and Errol Flynn." (Both were involved in paternity suits at the time.) After each chorus of "Pistol Packin' Mama," Garrigan would sing a different verse. "Two old maids were lyin' in bed. One at the bottom and one at the head. Oh my dear, isn't this queer. You're way down there and I'm way up here." The audience would howl.

One of my jobs, a full week, was at a place called Hurley's Log Cabin, where I worked as M.C. "Good evening, ladies and gentlemen," I'd say. "My name is Dallas Burrows. Harvard '48 . . . [pause] Yale nothing." There was no laughter. The audience was mostly men wearing lumber jackets, sitting at tables covered with Narragansett Beer bottles. The empties were never cleared from the table, it apparently being part of the macho mystique to leave evidence of the amount of beer that had been consumed in an evening.

To appreciate a joke like the one I'd told required a modicum of intelligence. The guys in the audience weren't stupid, far from it. It's just that they'd been trained to expect a certain form to the lines an M.C. used. ("My girlfriend is melancholy. She's got a head like a melon and a face like a collie.") I was starting to experiment with original humor, realizing that if I continued to steal Billy Garrigan's jingles, the best I could hope for was to wind up working in the same kinds of clubs as he did.

Victor Borge was one of the first comedians to record his comedy material. It was intellectual, like his phonetic punctuation routine, which gave sounds to commas, quotations marks and exclamation points. I memorized and stole some of Borge's stuff, rationalizing that Borge would never work in the places where I was employed. I did the pilfered routines to no discernable response. Luckily, I had my paper tree and the fake hypnotism to finish up the act with. They always brought down the house.

There was a four-piece band at Hurley's Log Cabin. (One of the jokes I used was: "This is really a *three*-piece band. The drummer is painted on the back wall.") The piano player in the band, a guy by the name of Val duVal, thought I was, as he put it, "the funniest thing since pay toilets." Every night he'd laugh it up for me, slapping his knee under the piano. The audience would listen to my jokes in silence and then look over at the piano player to see what was wrong with him.

Val duVal said that my routines were not going over with the audience because the opening joke didn't work. And that, he said, was because I didn't have a funny name. Each night, he would make up a different name for me to use. One night, he made up the name Roger Duck. I opened the show: "Good evening, ladies and gentlemen. My name is Roger Duck. Harvard '48 . . . Yale nothing." The clink of Narragansett Beer bottles was the only sound which broke the silence. Then someone yelled, "Bring out the stripper."

One night Val duVal made up the name Orson Bean. I used it, the joke got a laugh and my comedy routine killed the people for the first time. I was elated. As luck would have it, there was a local theatrical booking agent in the place that night, a fat guy named Bozo Zimbel. He came backstage after the show.

"You're alright, kid," he said. "I have a full week's work for you in Montreal." I was very excited.

"What's the money?" I asked.

"A hundred and twenty-five dollars less ten percent," he answered, "and you gotta pay your own traveling and living expenses."

"Jesus," I said. "It will cost me more than that to *do* it."

"Well," said Bozo Zimbel. "You gotta save up for these jobs."

The Montreal gig turned out to be a fiasco. The audience in the nightclub spoke nothing but French. Not even the hypnotism worked. When I whispered in the ears of my volunteers, they stared at me blankly. But I decided that the name Orson Bean had been lucky. When I got back to Boston another agent, Ettie MacKay, got me my big break. I went to work in a club called The College

Inn for an open-ended run at a hundred dollars a week.
The club was run by two guys named Rocky Paladino and
Irv Chipman, an Italian and a Jew. They were, as the
newspapers say, "reputed to have underworld connec-
tions." Rocky Paladino was a man of great charm, and he
took a liking to me. "Sit down, Oscar," he'd say. He
called me Oscar Beans. I don't know why.

Sitting at his table, I sometimes had a chance to meet
and observe other reputed members of the underworld
and their girlfriends. These were mostly former chorines,
slender, blonde, and of above-average intelligence. Occasionally a girlfriend would manage to marry her man.
When this happened, her life changed dramatically. She
got more respect but had less fun. Wives stayed home.
Girlfriends got to sit around with "the boys." They got to
drink, watch shows in the clubs and they were made love
to.

Sometimes they were treated badly, too. I once saw the
girlfriend of a guy named Vinnie slapped hard in the face
at a table down front in the club. I don't know what her
infraction was. "You fucking cunt," he told her. "You
douche bag." But a minute later he was holding her and
telling her he knew she wouldn't do whatever it was
again, and that everything was all right. It didn't occur to
anyone that his behavior was out of line. She was his
girlfriend and he was angry. But on another occasion, I
saw one of the boys use bad language in front of a wife.
There was silence and genuine embarrassment at the
table. I heard later that the chagrined guy had sent
flowers to the wife, with a note of apology. She was a
former chorine, like Vinnie's girl, but now she was
someone's wife.

Rocky wasn't too crazy about my jokes. The Victor
Borge phonetic punctuation routine left him cold. But he
loved to watch my hypnotism act. "That kid can make
anybody do anything," he'd laugh. Maybe my act
appealed to his sense of power. The year was 1949 and
the first of the big organized crime investigations was
underway in Washington. Frank Costello, the Godfather,

demanded and got his constitutional right not to have his
face appear on TV. The television producer came up with
the brilliant idea of zeroing in on his hands as he spoke.
They were immaculately groomed and constantly in
motion, drumming on the table, clasping and unclasping
or being pressed together at the fingertips. The idea put
television news coverage on the map.

Rocky Paladino was subpoenaed to go to Washington to
testify and be on TV. His appearance caused a sensation
in the club. Again and again in relaxed and authoritative
fashion, addressing the senators as equals, Rocky invoked
his constitutional rights.

"Mr. Paladino . . . On or about the evening of September 12th, 1943, did you encase the feet of one Salva-
tore Fatamiglio in cement and drop said Mr. Fatamiglio
in the Alewife Brook?"

"Senator, I respectfully decline to answer on the
grounds that I may tend to incriminate myself."

When Rocky came home, the club threw him a party.
He was a media star. I'd had a few drinks and felt
relaxed. I walked up to Rocky at a table where he sat
with some of his friends.

"Rocky," I asked, "is Costello really a killer?" There
was an awful silence. I had committed a gaffe. But Rocky
was feeling expansive and forgiving. "Beans," he said,
"Costello is no more of a killer than . . ." He paused and I
could see his lips about to form the words "*I* am."
Automatically, he edited himself. "*You* are," he finished.
"Sit down, Oscar. Have a drink."

There was a friend of Rocky Paladino's who hung
around the club. His name was Angie and he owned a
bar in Medford. He wore white-on-white ties over white-
on-white shirts, and he did not like me. Or maybe what
he didn't like was the obvious relish Rockie took in my
act.

"This kid can hypnotize anybody," Rocky told Angie
one night.

"Not me, he can't," said Angie.

"A hundred bucks says you're wrong."

As I was having my volunteers fall down and get stuck that night, an unasked-for assistant walked out onto the floor. "Make me fall down," growled Angie from Medford. The audience roared with laughter. Using the laugh to cover my secret instructions, I whispered to him, "It's all a gag. Do as I say." A terrible smile appeared on Angie's face as he slowly returned to his table.

After the show, Rocky called me to his office. "Beans," he said. "Oscar, my boy. What Angie tells me, it ain't true, is it?" I stared at the floor and scuffed it with my foot.

"Well, Rocky . . ."

"Get out," said Rocky and looked down at the papers on his desk. I didn't bother to ask whether I should pick up my final week's pay. I felt terrible. I hadn't exactly lied to him but I knew how disappointed in me he was. I called Ruthie to say goodbye and left the next morning for Philadelphia, feeling that I had peaked in Boston and that it was time to move on.

Philadelphia was another city where there was, back then, a full year's work to be booked in working class clubs scattered around the state: The Moose Club in Harrisburg, the V.F.W. in Altoona, the Peacock Cafe in Andalusia. I went to live at the Locust Hotel on 13th Street, and ate my dinner every evening at the Automat on Broad Street. My nightly budget was 25¢. A wide selection of delicious fresh vegetables could be bought at the steam table for a nickle each. I was a monetary vegetarian in those days. Two rolls and butter cost a nickle and lemonade was free. Horn and Hardart's hadn't planned it that way, but there was always a bowl of lemon wedges by the iced tea spigot, and customers could help themselves to ice water and sugar. I came to Philadelphia with $40 (better than Ben Franklin had done) and set about making myself known to the local agents.

My magic act was evolving into straight comedy. I had some new material in addition to the old stuff and was able, sometimes, to drop the hypnotism bit. After the

Rocky debacle, it always made me nervous. I was glad to have it to fall back on, though, at times when the verbal comedy wasn't playing.

I got to know some of the local comics, like Jay Weston and Arnie Sultan, who went on later to better things. After six months, I went to Baltimore for a while to work the stuff booked out of that city: clubs in Washington, D.C., and Pittsburgh. When I came back to Philadelphia, I ran into a comic I knew.

"I hate to tell you this," he said, "but your friend Jay Weston is a rat fink. While you were gone, he stole your Victor Borge routine."

At an American Legion Club in Johnstown, I worked with Little Frankie Mills. He was a skinny old guy with a few sparse strands of whispy white hair. His act, if you could call it that, consisted of a bottomless supply of stories, told in the old-fashioned manner, with embellishments of flowery language. He was like the Interlocutor in a minstrel show. The stories were mostly racist and slightly off color.

The audience of veterans and their wives adored him. He would stand motionless at the microphone and say, "A colored man walking down the street is accosted by a second Son of Ham who, it seems, has recently become a father. 'Well,' says the initial Ethiope to his dusky compatriot. 'I see where the stork has taken a Shine to your wife.'"

"Har, har, har," the audience would laugh, the vets slapping their knees . . . and when the laughter had crested so that he could be heard again, Little Frankie Mills would go on to his next story: "Two gentlemen of the Hebrew persuasion . . ."

I decided it was time to take a chance and move to New York. The audience participation was gone out of my act, along with most of the magic. I was doing all original material now. I hopped a bus to the Big Apple and checked in to a hotel on Eighth Avenue called The Capitol, where a number of variety performers stayed. It was up the block from the old Madison Square Garden. The second day I was in New York, in the middle of the afternoon, I strolled into a famous supper club called the Blue Angel and asked to see the boss. I didn't know it wasn't done that way. The boss's name was Max Gordon.

"I'm a comedian," I told him.

"Say something funny."

"Belly button."

A look of surprise and delight came over his face. "Come back tonight and I'll put you on. Then we'll talk."

After years of appearing at working class night clubs on the road, I finally had an audience of New York sophisticates. They went crazy for me. I wore a crew cut and a gray flannel suit. When I said Harvard '48, Yale nothing they roared. Max Gordon and his partner, Herbert Jacoby, signed me to a long-term contract for $125 a week. I had hit the outer fringes of the big time.

II

I remember Mr. Bartlett. In biology class he discusses the transformation of caterpillar into butterfly. "What's the process that goes on inside a cocoon?" he asks. "Has anyone ever seen a picture of the insect at the halfway point between caterpillar and butterfly? Does anyone know what it looks like?" No one has or does. The next week, Mr. Bartlett finds a cocoon in the woods and brings it to the classroom. We crowd around as he takes a razor blade and neatly slices it in two. The cocoon looks empty.

"There's nothing in there," says one of the kids.

"Oh, it's in there," says Mr. Bartlett. "It just doesn't have a shape right now. The living, organic material is spun right into the cocoon. Caterpillar is gone; butterfly is yet to come." We stare in wonder.

"Real transformation," says Mr. Bartlett, "means giving up one form before you have another. It requires the willingness to be *nothing* for a while."

Venice, California, 1987

III

I had moved out of the Capitol Hotel and was staying with the beautiful hatcheck girl from the Village Vanguard while I looked for a place of my own. The Vanguard, a subterranean crypt in Greenwich Village, was a jazz and comedy club owned by Max Gordon of the Blue Angel and I'd met the hatcheck girl when I appeared on the bill there. She was ten years older than I was and her name was Nola Chilton. It was a professional name. She'd been born Celia Traeger on the lower east side of Manhattan and her father peddled hot knishes from a pushcart there. She was not just a hatcheck girl but a brilliant stage director. In those days, a woman found it almost impossible to find employment as a director, no matter how good she was. Nola eventually moved to Israel, learned Hebrew and went on to become famous directing at the Habima, the National Theater of Israel.

But back then, she was a hatcheck girl and having an affair with me. She told me I should study acting and helped me enroll in a drama class. She said I should get in touch with my feelings and sent me to see a psychiatrist. During my first session with him, I talked about my childhood and my relationship with my mother. He asked me what I felt about her.

"Nothing," I replied.

"I think you might have some work to do," he said. I stayed with him for 10 years.

In the 1950s I became, for practical purposes, house comic at the Blue Angel, working there at least six months out of every year. My act consisted of character routines, which I'd written during my years on the road: two Chinese guys ordering American food, a Martian talking about the trouble he'd had with his landlady over his kid's pet goo-goo, an Aussie on trial for having an affair with an ostrich. Broadway producers came into the club, saw these acting vignettes and I started to get parts in shows. I was cast in *John Murray Anderson's Almanac*, the last of the great tits-and-feathers musical reviews. When the curtain came down at the theater, I'd hop on my bicycle and peddle across town, dodging traffic, arriving in time for my midnight show at the Blue Angel. New York nightlife was jumping. Edith Piaf sang at the Versailles; Milton Berle and Frank Sinatra starred at The Copa.

Ed Sullivan came into the Blue Angel one night and saw my show. He liked it and called the next morning to book me on his program. I became one of his regulars. Ed would say, "And now, here is my young crew-cut-headed friend Orson Bean." Ed never learned to read cue cards. Once, when the Singing Nun was on his show, he said: "Because Sister Dominique is a member of a religious order, she cannot accept financial recompense, so in lieu of payment, we are presenting her convent with a Jew." He stopped, appeared startled, peered at the cue card again and then said, "I'm sorry . . . a Jeep."

When I wasn't working at the Blue Angel, I frequently entertained at Max Gordon's other club, the Village Vanguard. Max had a unique ability to spot talent. I was

there when Harry Belafonte and Johnny Mathis performed their acts for the first time in public at the
Vanguard. "Not bad," said Max. "A little more experience
and they'll be OK," and he hired them. He flew Sho-
shana Damari, "the Israeli Nightingale," over from Tel
Aviv to sing at the club. I became infatuated with her, as
did every other male employee of the establishment.

This included Walter the waiter, who handled the limited food service in typical New York fashion.

"Gimme a hot turkey sandwich," says a customer.

"We ain't got it," says Walter.

"OK," says the customer. "How about a hot chicken
sandwich?"

"Schmuck," says Walter. "Would I refuse you a hot turkey sandwich if we had chicken?"

In actual fact, "the chef," as he was called, a short
order cook whose name I can't remember, would go to
the market once a week and return carrying the carcass,
wrapped in wax paper, of an enormous (unidentified)
bird. This he would boil in a huge galvanized caldron and
carve to order from it, as the week went on, hot turkey
sandwiches, hot chicken sandwiches, veal cutlets, almost
anything a customer might desire.

In the last few years of his life, Lenny Bruce appeared
at the Vanguard several times and I was able to sit in the
back of the club to worship and learn from this great,
self-destructive genius.

There was a drugstore called Hanson's on Seventh
Avenue and 51st Street where New York variety performers hung out. Now that I was one of them, I hung out
there too. One day when I was in there, I heard my name
called by a familiar voice. I looked around and it was Little Frankie Mills.

"Hi Frankie," I said. "What are you doing in New
York?" I knew he only worked the sticks.

"Let's have a cup of coffee and a piece of pie and I'll
tell you," said Frankie. He sat down next to me and I
ordered coffee and pie for two from the counterman.

"I'm working the bar at the Taft Hotel across the street," he said. I looked through Hanson's window at the old hotel on the other side of Seventh Avenue.

"But they don't have shows at the Taft."

"You're tellin' me. The place is jam-packed with Shriners, in town for the convention. Here, look at this." He snapped open a brown leather traveling case he had with him. It was filled with armbands, badges, caps, hats and fezzes. They had insignia on them from organizations like the Knights of Columbus, the Knights of Pythias, the Veterans of Foreign Wars and various other patriotic and Shriner groups.

"Whenever I'm between layoffs," he said, using a stock comic line, "I pick up a copy of Billboard and find out where there's a convention going on. The Shriners are in New York this week . . . next week, the Legion is in Pittsburgh. I hop a Greyhound, put on the right hat and show up in the right hotel. I go into the bar, invest in a C.C. and soda and start telling a few stories. After I get 'em going real good, have the whole place rocking, I mention that I haven't checked into the hotel yet, that the wife is at home and I'm attending the convention on my own. One of the guys will always suggest I bunk in with him, share his suite and all for free, and I never pay for a meal or a drink the whole three days.

"Well," he said, "It's a living. The clubs sure ain't steady any more and it beats the hell out of heavy lifting." He finished his pie, thanked me for it, popped on his fez and headed across the street to the Taft.

In mid-town Manhattan, at 48th Street and Fifth Avenue, I found an apartment. The rent was $120 a month. I swallowed hard and decided I'd have to pay it. My affair with Nola had run its course. My television career had begun to boom. In addition to the Sullivan appearances, I worked as an actor on all the live dramatic programs: *Playhouse 90*, *Studio One*, etc. CBS hired me to host a variety show called *The Blue Angel*. They ran it for 26 weeks and then produced a pilot for *The Orson*

Bean Show. I was riding high.

By the summer of 1956, I had money enough to rent a vacation cottage in the town of Ocean Beach on Fire Island. I was due to go into rehearsal in September to co-star on Broadway with Jayne Mansfield and Walter Matthau in *Will Success Spoil Rock Hunter,* so I felt OK about taking the summer off. Fire Island, in those days, was a haven for actors, writers and broadcasting people. A few houses from mine, Mel Brooks sat on Carl Reiner's porch, where they made up routines like the 2000-year-old man. Around the corner lived a radio broadcaster named John Henry Faulk. He had the top-rated afternoon show on the local CBS affiliate. We didn't need an introduction; as S.J. Perelman has written: "There are no strangers in the aristocracy of success."

John was from Texas and a man of inordinate charm. He had a beautiful wife, three kids and a pet goat. The goat would come when he called, follow him down the sidewalk and do everything but carry home the paper. John told wonderful stories about the poor people of Texas. He'd do them in dialect and there was one about a little girl who dreamed of some day owning a pair of shoes which always left me in tears.

On Friday and Saturday nights, groups of performers and broadcasting people would get together at Johnny's house, drawn by his personality like gnats to jam. Mrs. Faulk would serve drinks, the tanned and happy children would clamor to stay up longer, the goat would run in and out of the house and the guests would talk politics.

In those days, the communications industry was in the grips of a blacklist. A book named *Red Channels* had been published, naming the actors, directors, and writers its editors thought might be Communists, and the people on the list were finding it hard to get work. *Red Channels* also put out a news bulletin every few weeks called *Counterattack,* which constantly added more names. A super-patriot grocer from Syracuse started writing to the big food companies like Heinz and Campbell, telling them they need no longer send him their soups if they sponsored programs with any of the people from *Red Channels* or *Counterattack* on them.

The television and radio performers' union (AFTRA) was ripped apart over the issue of blacklisting. For years, in movies and radio, back in the forties, a group of Communist producers and directors had hired nothing but left-wing actors. This had resulted in a hardcore bunch of bitter conservative (sometimes reactionary) actors who were burning for revenge by the time the McCarthy hysteria hit the industry. The Left had also divided the union by pushing it to take stands on non-theatrical issues like the trial of the Trenton Six, etc. Things were so badly split back then that when actors came to union meetings, they'd sit on the right or left side of the hall to show their political position. The right wing controlled the board of directors, the left wing packed meetings (and hooted at the board) and the rest of the membership was scared or apathetic. As a result, the union took no stand against blacklisting, thus, in effect, supporting it.

The summer of 1956 was a hot one, both meteorologically and politically. In Maine, agents of the federal government entered the estate of an accused Communist, the brilliant and eccentric psychiatrist Wilhelm Reich. Using sledge hammers, they smashed his so-called Orgone boxes. In New York, other agents of the government shoveled piles of his books into furnaces in the city incinerator in downtown Manhattan. This took place 25 years after the Nazi book burning in Berlin.

At Johnny Faulk's house on Fire Island, the blacklist became the topic of conversation on weekend evenings. The Hollywood Ten had been driven out of the movies and big stars and well-known supporting players were through in the business. Even Lucille Ball made headlines when someone dug up the fact that she'd once voted for a Communist candidate for Congress. Desi Arnez came to the rescue by calling a press conference to deny his wife was a Red.

"You know Lucy," he said. "She didn't even know who the hell she was voting for." So the smartest business woman in Hollywood saved herself by acting like the dizzy dame she played on her own series.

One week that summer, the Un-American Activities Committee came to New York and subpoenaed a bunch of actors it said were Reds, Pinkos or Dupes. A meeting was called at Carnegie Hall to protest the committee's trip to New York and I volunteered to appear at it. While I was waiting backstage to go on, a left-wing friend spotted me.

"What the hell are you doing here," he said. "The place is lousy with FBI guys, taking everybody's name down." Undeterred, I went on and did one of my routines from the Sullivan Show.

Night after night that summer on Fire Island, John Henry Faulk held forth on the evils of the blacklist. People within the union were cooperating with *Counterattack* to "rid the airwaves of Reds."

"Honey," Johnny would say in his charming Texas drawl, "don't kid yourself. These people are fascists and dangerous. They'll sit there grinnin' like egg-suckin' dawgs, all friendly-like, but they'll kill us and they'll kill the country."

Galvanized, a group of us decided to form a slate of candidates and run for union office. Maybe we could destroy the blacklist. We'd call ourselves the Middle of the Road Slate, and be politically neither left nor right. Word of our plan spread through the industry. Famous performers like Jack Paar and Tony Randall joined us; so did Charles Collingwood, the news correspondent. We were as excited as hell.

We gathered at Johnny's New York apartment to finalize our plans. When the meeting was called to order, somebody said, "You know, we've really got to offer the membership a clean slate. We shouldn't be running any of the tired old faces who've been involved in left wing politics, and I hate to say it but a few of us have been." There was an embarrassed pause and then a fairly well known actor spoke up.

"Well," he said, "I guess that's my cue to bow out. It would have been fun, and I'd like to go along for the ride, but I have been a joiner in my day, and I agree that the slate should be completely clean." There were a few cries of "No", but reason prevailed and his name was regretfully withdrawn. One other performer said that he too had better back off, and then I opened my mouth to confess my appearance at Carnegie Hall. There was a pause and someone said, "Anything else?"

"No," I said, "except I voted for Adlai Stevenson." There was laughter all around and Johnny said, "Hell, honey, you're as pure as a Baptist minister's six-year-old daughter. They can't get you for that one little thing. Stick with us, honey."

I was very relieved and we ran our slate. *The New York Times* wrote an article about us, and when the election was held we won a smashing victory. Charles Collingwood became president of the New York local of AFTRA, I became first vice president and John Henry Faulk was elected second veep. *The Times* and everyone else agreed the blacklist had been dealt a serious blow and we were all as happy as clams.

A few weeks later, my phone rang. I recognized the voice right away. It was Ed Sullivan. I was booked to be on his show the following Sunday and figured he was calling to discuss what material I'd do.

"Orson," he said. "Have you heard about the *Counterattack* bulletin?"

"What do you mean?" I could feel the blood draining out of my face.

"They've cited you in today's issue and I'm afraid that means the bookings are out. In fact, I won't be able to use you on the show at all anymore." I felt sick. "If you tell anyone I called, I'll have to deny it, you know."

"I understand. Can you say what they said about me?"

"Sure. They say you appeared at some Communist meeting and did a skit ridiculing the House Un-American Activities Committee."

"I did one of the dumb routines I've done on your show."

"Well," said Ed Sullivan, "I'll help you when I can."

He hung up. I sat there thunderstruck. How could they nail me for one lousy appearance? How could they say I was a Communist or a Communist dupe or a Communist sympathizer because of one lousy protest meeting?

I pulled myself together and started frantically making phone calls. Charlie Collingwood was in trouble too. *Counterattack* had condemned him for writing a critical letter to the Un-American Activities Committee. CBS was meeting to decide what to do about him. Finally, I got a look at the new issue of the news bulletin.

It was a condemnation of our slate and it asked rhetorically just how middle of the road we were. To answer the question, it listed the three top officers, Collingwood, me and Faulk. Starting with John Henry it said: "How about Faulk? What is his public record? According to *The Daily Worker* of April 22, 1946 . . ." I read with wonder as it went on and on: Johnny at "Headline Cabaret," sponsored by Stage for Action, officially designated as a Communist front; Johnny appearing with Paul Robeson at the Communist Jefferson School; Johnny sending greetings to *People's Songs*, a Red publication; Johnny as U.S. sponsor of the "American Continental Congress for Peace" in Mexico City; Johnny at "Showtime for Wallace," staged by Progressive Citizens of America, a Communist front.

When the bulletin was finally through with Johnny, it turned to the other two officers on the slate. It said that I'd appeared at the protest meeting and it mentioned Charlie's letter. By themselves, the charges against Collingwood and me would have been worth zip. Lumped in with all they had to say about Faulk, they added up to a grim picture. I was appalled. How could *Counterattack* have made up such stuff about Johnny? I was sure it couldn't be true or he wouldn't have jeopardized us all by running on the slate.

I dashed up to his office at CBS. "It's not true, is it, John? You didn't appear at those places, did you?"

"Oh, honey," he said. "What does it matter? Don't you see those people are fascists? If they didn't have something on us, they'd have made something up."

Overnight, from being the hottest young comic on television, I stopped working. CBS shelved *The Orson Bean Show* pilot. I saw actor acquaintances of mine cross the street when they saw me coming so they wouldn't have to say hello. I was even snubbed by the doorman at CBS. Charlie Collingwood held on by the skin of his teeth with the support of Ed Murrow and others. The network sent him overseas to be its London correspondent until the controversy died down. Johnny Faulk lost his radio show. He hired attorney Louis Nizer to sue the Syracuse grocer and he won a multi-million dollar award. But in a soap-operatic twist, the grocer died while the jury was still deliberating and it turned out that his estate had no money.

My luck was better. *Will Success Spoil Rock Hunter* became a hit (the blacklist never had much effect on the theater). The part I played was that of a no-talent screen writer who sells 10 percent of his soul to a diabolical agent for the love of a Marilyn-like movie star. Jayne Mansfield was one of hundreds of beautiful blond women who had auditioned for the role. She had never acted on the professional stage before, but was cast the minute the producers saw her. Every night in the play it was my job to make love to Jayne. Cab drivers would yell at me: "For this you get paid?"

Mansfield was adorable. She was purée of movie magazine. She did not want to be an actress, she wanted to be a star. We liked each other. I'd rap on her dressing room door.

"Who is it?"

"It's Orson."

"Ooo, Orsie. Come in." She'd be sitting at her make-up table completely and spectacularly naked. "Sit down, Orsie." I never knew where to look.

Walter Matthau was also in the cast of the show. Walter had a reputation as an actor's actor. He had been in twenty-odd Broadway plays, all of which had closed in a few weeks or so. This was his first long-run hit. He didn't care for Mansfield as much as I did.

"The bitch upstages me every time," he complained.

"She's just an amateur," I told him. "She only does it by accident."

"Oh yeah? Well, how come she's never even once by accident *down*staged me?"

Martin Gabel was the devil who purchases part of my soul. He didn't care for Mansfield either. "To think that I," he grumbled, "who have played Cassius with Orson Welles, should be reduced to appearing in this tawdry comedy with that tart." Martin had aristocratic ways; they were an affectation with him. When the show had been running a few months, I invited him to dinner on our night off. "My dear fellow," he said, "working together does not constitute a social introduction," and he didn't come. I couldn't stay mad at Martin, though; he was too lovable. A lovable snob. One night he was sitting on a stool at his favorite bar, wearing a dolorous expression. His foot was propped up on the bar stool next to his. He explained his situation to a drinking companion who happened in. "I have the gout, you see," he sighed.

"Well Martin," said his friend. "You are finally developing the diseases of your pretensions."

A former musical revue comic named Harry Clark was also in the show. His role was the ruthless head of the movie studio where Jayne Mansfield was a star. He had a hilarious scene where he listened to a lugubrious story told by Martin Gabel and wept real tears. Marlon Brando came to see the play one night. He had recently starred on Broadway in *A Streetcar Named Desire* and was the toast of the town. Marlon studied at the Actors Studio where the question young thespians asked one another when they had to express emotion in a scene was, "What did you *use?*" For instance, if an actor had to weep, he might "use" the memory of the death of his childhood pet dog. Actors Studio actors were supposed to "feel it."

Marlon was an acquaintance of mine; we had a few mutual friends. He came backstage after the performance.

"Do you want to meet Jayne Mansfield?" I asked him.

"No," said Marlon. "Introduce me to that guy Harry Clark." We climbed up three flights of stairs to Harry's dressing room. I knocked on the door and he opened it.

"This is my friend Marlon Brando, Harry."

"Oh Jeeze, Marlon. What an honor."

"Mr. Clark," said Marlon. "That scene of yours in the second act was very impressive. Not only was it hilarious, it was genuinely moving. Would you mind telling me, what did you *use*?"

"Huh? Whaddaya mean, Marlon?"

"What did you *use* to *cry*?"

"Oh. I gotcha, Marlon. Aw sure, I'll tell ya. This is good and you're welcome to use it yourself: the lights off stage left are very bright, so during that whole long scene I never blink. It really makes your eyes water." Marlon left the theater mumbling to himself. *Will Success Spoil Rock Hunter* ran on Broadway for just over a year.

In time, as the political climate eased, Ed Sullivan kept his promise and was able to book me on his program again. This broke the ice and little by little I began to work on TV once more. As I look back on the period, there was an irony to my experience: the main reason I went to that protest meeting at Carnegie Hall was that I was in love with a girl on the organizing committee. Well actually, she wasn't on the committee, her boyfriend was. He was a blacklisted actor whose martyrdom, I believed, gave him stature in her eyes. Now that I'd been black-listed too, I seemed better able to compete with my rival. I wooed and eventually won the lady.

Rain Winslow was a gifted actress and dancer. She had changed her name for professional purposes. When the former Jacqueline deSibour married the former Dallas Burrows, her name became Rain Bean. We should have taken that as an omen: the marriage did not last. When the beautiful baby daughter she presented me with was a year old, Rain fell tête over talons in love with a French-man. Caught in a romantic maelstrom, she ran off with him to French Equatorial Africa, leaving me with the baby, the sheets, the silverware and selected pieces of

furniture. At the time, I was annoyed. Fortunately I was
still in analysis (after 10 years). My psychiatrist offered his
best professional judgment on the matter. "What a bum-
mer," he said.

Back before it was the trendy thing to do, I became a
male, single parent. Prior to leaving, Rain had hired a
seventeen-year-old Irish immigrant girl named Bridie
o'Dowd to live with us as a maid. She stayed on with me
and my daughter, Michele, and the three of us set up
housekeeping in an apartment overlooking the East River.
Bridie had "a rosy cheeked, peasanty, droit-du-seigneur
beauty and a body that made Raquel Welch look like a
rake."* "It was an odd situation: a horny, miserable
bachelor, a year-and-a-half-old baby girl and this ravish-
ing Irish teenager occupying a luxury flat on Manhattan's
East Side."**

I embarked on a year of emotional hibernation, sitting
in my chair by the window that looked out on the river,
playing old Sinatra records ("Are You Lonesome
Tonight?") and feeling sorry for myself. My self-pity was
assuaged by the joy my little daughter brought into my
life as we became closer and closer. Once again, a job
came to the rescue when I needed it most. David Merrick
hired me to play one of the leads in a Comden and
Greene/Jule Styne musical called *Subways Are for Sleeping*. The show had a big advance sale. Audiences liked it,
but it opened on Broadway to negative reviews.

Merrick was furious. He swore revenge on the critics
and he got it. He found men with the same names as the
important newspaper critics: Howard Taubman a cab
driver, Walter Kerr a tree surgeon, etc. He put quotes
from these bogus critics in an ad and submitted it to the
four morning papers. The *Times, News* and *Mirror*
caught the gag and turned the ad down. But the *Herald-
Tribune* was asleep at the switch and published it.

---

* The way I described her in my 1971 book, *Me and the Orgone*, and I
feel no need to improve on it.
    ** Ibid. (I've always wanted to be able to use Ibid.)

Merrick was wild with joy. He ran backstage after the show waving a copy of the next morning's paper and danced a terrible jig like Hitler had danced in the Ardennes. "Revenge is wonderful," he sang.

The practical joke made every newspaper in the country. *Time* magazine gave it a full page. *Subways Are For Sleeping* turned into a hit. I had a show-stopping number in it called "I Just Can't Wait Till I See You With Clothes On," which earned me a Tony nomination. Aside from that, what I remember from the production is being taken by a group of the chorus kids to the Peppermint Lounge and becoming one of the first people to learn the Twist. The sixties were upon us.

But what I felt most grateful to the show for was the friendship I formed with one of its stars, Sydney Chaplin. The period was a bleak one for me and the evenings I spent with Syd after work, in the myriad bars of Manhattan, getting to know his friends like Hank Fonda and Gene Kelly and listening to him recount his hilarious view of life, helped me get through it and come out the other side intact.

Sydney Chaplin had (has) one of the great, creative dirty mouths in history, ranking with that of James Joyce or Henry Miller. Such was his ingenuousness, though, that people virtually never took offense. To be called a "chicken kisser" or a "moose fucker" and *like* it, was to have been exposed to the special charm of Sydney Chaplin.

When *Subways Are For Sleeping* closed, I had an experience that left a deep impression on me. Michele had just turned three and arrangements had been made for her to fly to Paris and stay with her mother for a month. Bridie was to go along and be with her on the trip. She asked if she and Michele could stop on the way and spend some time with her parents, who lived in Dingle, a beautiful little town west of Tralee. I said sure. Then, after they'd left, I decided to join them, enjoy a few days in Ireland and deliver Bridie and Michele to Paris myself.

I arrived at Shannon Airport at five A.M., went through customs, picked up my rental car and started off on the four-hour drive to the Dingle peninsula, the westernmost spot in Ireland. A friend, Michael McCourt, who worked in one of the watering holes I frequented with Sydney, had originally come from the town of Limerick. "It's right on the road from Shannon to Dingle," he told me. "Here. Take this twenty and give it to Blackie, the bartender in McGill's Grill. I borrowed it from him 15 years ago and I'm sure he's forgotten about it. Tell him I said, 'Here's your twenty bucks back. Stop hounding me.'"

I arrived in Limerick, a gray, sodden, inhospitable, working class town of no particular character, at 6:30 A.M. The weather was cold and clammy and there was a drizzle in the air. I hadn't been able to sleep more than an hour or so on the plane and was exhausted and jet-lagged. The town wasn't open yet; there was no place even to sit down and have a cup of coffee. I parked my car and walked the streets, looking for McGill's. A man passed me, wearing overalls, a heavy woolen sweater and a laborer's cap. I asked him if he knew the place. When he answered, I couldn't understand his thick accent, but I followed the direction he pointed in and found McGill's, a run-down establishment of the White Rose variety. OPEN AT TEN A.M. the sign in the window read.

I was chilled, wet, hungry, exhausted and miserable . . . and had three hours to kill. I could have told Michael McCourt I hadn't been able to find Blackie, and given him his twenty back, but I cared about him and didn't want to do that. I wandered the town, wasting time, looking in shop windows at unfamiliar consumer goods. I started to feel sorry for myself. I missed Rain and the prospect of seeing her in Paris when I dropped off Michele upset me.

I checked my watch. It was just past seven. I found a little diner which had just opened and ordered fried eggs and bacon. The eggs were like concrete and the bacon was lank and greasy. I chewed the toast and drank two cups of "white coffee." It was now seven thirty and I only had two and a half hours to kill until McGill's opened. I walked the streets of Limerick again, desperately lonely, then stopped in front of a Rent-a-Telly store and stared at the Phillips black-and-white TV sets in the window.

Out of nowhere, peace of mind suddenly descended upon me, a feeling of pure, unadulterated joy. My body became light, my mind cleared, my senses were totally in touch with where I was at that moment: standing in the drizzle in a strange town in a foreign country with no place to go and nothing to do for the next two hours. I looked around. The town now seemed picturesque and beautiful. The few people passing on the street, who had previously appeared aloof if not downright hostile, were smiling at me and touching their caps as they went by. It was as if a fairy godmother had brushed the scene with a magic wand. I had never felt so happy, secure and content in my life. It seemed as if I knew and liked everyone in the world and everyone in the world knew and liked me. I wandered through Limerick, marveling at what a wonderful place it was. I couldn't get enough of it. I considered retiring from show business and moving there.

The sensation lasted for an hour and a half, then slowly began to fade. I desperately tried to hold on to it. I didn't go back to feeling miserable, but a low-grade anxiety seemed to drift in and blanket my sense of well being, filtering out most of the pleasure. At ten o'clock, McGill's Grill opened and Blackie O'Malley stood behind the bar. "The twenty from Michael McCourt," he said when I handed it to him. "Well, it's about time. Will you have one on the house?"

When I returned home, my agent had good news for me. I had been hired to co-star with Paul Ford and Maureen O'Sullivan in *Never Too Late*, a comedy to be staged by George Abbott, one of the theater's great directors. The play turned out to be a smash hit, which kept me gainfully employed for two years. By then I had become, as well, a regular panelist on *To Tell the Truth*, a CBS network game show.

On the non show biz front, I finished up my analysis (mainly, I believe, because the doctor became sick of listening to my stuff and wanted to clear some time to listen to other people's stuff). I engaged in no self-improvement for a while, then went into Orgone Therapy with Dr. Elsworth Baker, a disciple of the late Wilhelm Reich (of Orgone Box fame). It was a physical regime, where I'd lie naked on a couch and breathe, while the doctor pummelled me in an attempt to break down my "armoring."

It was at this point in my life, emotionally primed and ready, that I met the woman who was to become my next wife. It happened, of course, in a bar. The place was called Sparks' Pub. My friend Michael McCourt knew the bartender and had taken me there after my performance in *Never Too Late* that night. The phenomenon of East Side Singles Bars was just getting started in 1963. Sparks' Pub was one of the first. Most of the establishments on the upper east side of New York City catered to a German, Czechoslovakian or Lithuanian clientele. They contained no Boston ferns, were meant for plain pipe-rack drinking. Sparks' Pub, recently The Krakow, had been newly acquired and ferned.

I stood at the bar holding a Dewar's scotch and water. That was what I drank in those days.

"Look at that girl in the yellow sweater," I said to Michael McCourt. (You didn't have to say woman back then.) "She's a knockout." The knockout was sitting at a table next to the juke box, with another beauty and a red-faced guy.

"That's Don Sparks at the table with her," said Michael. "He owns the joint."

"Do you know him?"

"We've said hello. Whitey says he's OK. Do you want me to introduce you?"

"I'd sure like to meet that girl."

Michael caught the bartender's eye and signalled him over.

"Whitey, this is my friend, Orson Bean."

Whitey wiped his hand on a bar rag and offered it to me. "My mother watches you every day on *To Tell the Truth*," he said.

"Thanks," I answered, deciding to take it as a compliment.

"Look," said Michael. "When you get a chance, introduce him to Sparks, will you? He wants to meet one of the dames at his table." The bartender made a leave-it-to-me sign and moved away. My heart was pounding. I couldn't stop staring at her. As I watched, she got up from the table to visit the ladies' room, going toward the back of the restaurant.

A few minutes later, Don Sparks, the genial boniface, was smiling and pumping my hand.

"Well, Orson Bean," he said. "I'm glad you found us. I hear your play is great. I've been meaning to catch it. Hello there, young Michael. So you brought the man up here, did you? Whitey, a round for the boys. Would you care to join us at the table?"

"He'd care to," said Michael. "I'll enjoy my free drink right here, thanks."

Don Sparks was leading me to her. I carried my glass. There was an unoccupied chair next to hers. Her girl friend looked up as we approached and gave a big smile to Don Sparks. Then *she* looked up, first at Sparks, then at me. Her eyes appraised me as we approached. I couldn't tell whether she liked what she saw or not. My mouth felt dry.

"This is Orson Bean, ladies. I'm sure you've seen him on *What's My Line*." (I decided to let it pass.) "This is Sheila and her friend . . . I'm sorry, dear, what's your name again?"

We had made a date that night, exchanged phone numbers and then I had split. A cab had been cruising by on the street outside and I had hailed it. My place was only a few blocks away, but I hadn't felt like walking. I'd wanted to get home quickly, for some reason, to sit in my chair and think about what had happened. Bridie was

waiting up when I arrived at the apartment, shortly
before one A.M. "Oh, Mr. Bean . . ." She always insisted
on calling me Mr. Bean. "I was hopin' you wouldn't get
home too late. Would it be alright if I went out for a
while? Herself is fast asleep, of course, and my sister Mary
just called from the Jaeger House." It was an 86th Street
establishment patronized by Irish-American elevator
operators, nannies and cops.

"Of course, Bridie." It was what usually happened and
it really was fine with me. She was young and seemed to
get by on very little sleep and always remain cheery.
Michele loved her and I was glad Rain had hired her
before she had cut out. She gave me a kiss on the cheek as
she flew past.

"Thank you, Mr. Bean." Pausing at the door, she
looked back at me and made a sniffing sound. "You've
been rubbin' up against someone who smells very nice."

I laughed. "You may meet her, Bridie. We've got a date
tomorrow night."

"And you'll be bringin' her back here?" Bridie tolerated
the succession of women who had begun to pass through
the apartment.

"I don't know, dear. We'll see. This one is different. I
think she's special." She continued on out the door. I
locked it behind her and tiptoed into Michele's room.
There was a little Donald Duck nightlight stuck into a
wall socket near her crib, casting a faint glow over it. I
looked down at her and felt flooded with love. Then she
whimpered in her sleep and a sudden sense of sadness took
me over. My little girl was growing up without a mother.
I didn't blame Rain anymore; she'd done what she had
had to do. Her karma was her karma and Michele's was
hers and mine was mine. Then the woman I'd just met
popped into my mind and the sadness evaporated.

I left my daughter's bedroom, walked into the tiny
kitchen of my apartment and selected a glass from the
cupboard over the sink. I removed a handful of ice cubes
from the freezer and dropped them into the glass. Then I
poured a dollop of scotch onto it and filled it up with tap

water. I carried it to the dark brown corduroy armchair by the large window that looked out onto the river, sat down and took a sip of the drink. I felt excited; it seemed as if my life was about to undergo a change. I gazed at the river, replaying the evening in my mind.

The phone was ringing. I snapped out of my reverie and tore my eyes away from the river. Carrying my empty scotch glass into the kitchen, I lifted the receiver from its cradle on the wall.

"Hello?"

"Hello. I just wanted to say I'm really glad we met tonight." Pure pleasure flooded through me.

"That's so sweet of you. It makes me feel really good. I'm glad we met too."

"Well, I'll wait for your call and see you tomorrow night."

"Don't eat anything between now and then. I'm taking you to Orsini's and their cooking is terrific."

She chuckled. "Don't worry. It's not a problem. The only food in the house is half a box of cornflakes and there's no milk."

"Goodnight, Carolyn."

"Goodnight, Orson."

I hung up the phone and laughed out loud with happiness. Then I switched off the lights and went into the bathroom to get ready for bed.

IV

What the hell is time? Here I am in the future writing this book, looking back on the beginnings of a new relationship. Carolyn and I are a thing of the past and I'm getting all excited over our date tomorrow in a restaurant that no longer even exists.

"Now" is the only time there ever really is. The past and the future exist only in my mind, the one as memory, the other as anticipation. Real time is an on-going succession of continuous moments of now. It's now *now*. And *now* it's now. And *now*. I can imagine the future, for example, thirty seconds from now (as good a future as any.) But when the thirty seconds go by, it's *now* . . . the same now it was thirty seconds ago when I called the current now the future. Now, I think of that now as past. But it's all the same now and it's filled with love and healing.

Orson can wonder what he'll be doing next Thursday: "What will I do then?" But the time never comes when he leaps out of bed and cries. "At last, it's *then!*" It will be *now* next Thursday . . . the same now it is now.

When I am totally, wholeheartedly engrossed in this moment, I am in touch with everything there is: I am fulfilled, content, at peace. The Eastern sages say, "Let go of fear and of anger and of desire . . . and you will have everything."

I'm so excited about our date tomorrow night in Orsini's.

Venice, California, 1987

V

Orsini's on West 56th Street was owned and operated by the Orsini brothers: Elio, plain and plain spoken, an Italian family man, and Armando, handsome and debonaire, a sophisticated charmer. On nights when Elio managed the restaurant, he sat quietly at a corner table, dispensing orders to waiters, rising occasionally to make forays into the kitchen. But when Armando was in charge he worked the room, welcoming diners at the door, joining them at their tables, lingering long enough to make customers feel like members of an exclusive club.

His tailoring was European-impeccable: conservative gray suit, spread collar, Countess Mara tie and foulard. He kissed the hand of each female who entered, then gazed into her eyes for an instant as if expressing regret for what might have been.

The restaurant was darkly lit, ideal for courting, with a love seat for two at each table. A painting on the wall at the center of the long narrow main room (the building was a converted brownstone) depicted a turn-of-the-century nude peering demurely at the beholder, her hand chastly covering her mound of Venus.

I had been introduced to this most romantic of restaurants by Sydney Chaplin.

"Noel's coming with us tonight, Orson, old buddy," he had told me that evening. He was married to the beautiful French actress and dancer, Noel Adam, and had taught her all the English she knew: "I don' mind 'e go wiz you to drink every night, Orson, because I know 'e is, 'ow you say *faiseful* . . . zat 'e will never make le fuckage wiz anozer woman."

"Before long you're bound to have a new lady in your life," Syd had said, "and you're going to have to know about Orsini's." So the three of us had gone there.

Our arrival was a cause for rejoicing among the staff. Everyone adored Sydney.

"Manager! Where's the manager!" he cried as we were shown to our table. "The dame in the picture with her hand on her snatch is engaging in self-abuse. This is shocking!"

The maître d' roared with delight. "Ah, Signor Chaplin. We'll have the painting retouched by the next time you're here."

Late in the evening, the talk had become increasingly scatalogical and apparently too loud, for we looked up to behold a businessman, a red-faced Shriner from the midwest, hovering over our table, come to complain of the bad language.

"I'd like you people to know," he announced, turning to indicate a gray-haired lady sitting two tables away, "that I happen to be here with my wife."

Up from his chair leapt Sydney, pointing at the beautiful Noel and crying, "What the hell do you think *this* is, a pile of shit?"

And now, here I was in Orsini's again with my future ex-wife. When I'd picked her up in the cab that night after my evening performance (it was Saturday and I'd done a matinee as well), I'd been staggered once more by her fresh-faced American beauty. She had long, lustrous

brown hair (steam-ironed fashionably straight), a sprin-
kling of freckles on her nose, a generous mouth set in a
determined jaw bespeaking a stubbornness which possibly
matched my own, and a direct look in her eyes that sent
shivers up my spine. She was small of stature but with the
curves of a college cheerleader. Most important, she
seemed self-possessed, in charge of herself (not likely to
stick her head in the oven).

We were nestled in one of Orsini's comfy love seats.
Armando was on duty that night and had given us the full
treatment at the door.

"Armando, I'd like you to meet Carolyn Maxwell."

"Ah, che bella signorina." A smootch on the hand, a
quick look into her eyes, followed by a congratulatory
glance at me. Then the best table in the house (I'd called
in the afternoon to make sure), a bottle of Ruffino Riserva
Gold (unpretentiously excellent), a beginner's plate of perfect, hot, crisp zuchini fritti . . . and I could tell that the
lady was on the way to being impressed.

In the center of each table was a glass holding individually wrapped bread sticks (thinner than the Duchess of
Windsor), which snapped when you broke them. Each
lady's menu sported a tiny red rose; there was no mention
of money on it.

Settling my arm on the back of the love seat behind
Carolyn, I leaned close, pointing out selections on the
menu. Her perfume, combined with her personal scent,
spun in my nostrils.

"I'd suggest we share an order of Fettuccine
Alfredo . . . they do it better than Alfredo's in Rome [I
wasn't above a little restaurant dropping], then picatta
limone, the simplest and best of the veal dishes, some
fresh spinach sauteed in butter and a small salad of aru-
gala. How does that sound to you?'

She regarded me with her limpid, greenish eyes. "That
sounds just fine to me. Particularly after a lunch of dry
cornflakes."

Isador, my favorite of the maître d's, attended to our
needs, snapping commands at the waiters, who snapped

commands at the bus boys, who scuttled like land crabs in
and out of the kitchen. The fettuccine was prepared with
great ceremony over the flames on a cart in front of our
table, the wine was poured and repoured, the dinner was
superb and for dessert we had hot, whipped zabaglione
(which Sydney Chaplin had once called "angel come.").

As we broke bread (sticks), we got to know each other.

"Do you still have family back home," I asked? She
had. A mother, an aunt and uncle, some cousins. No
father. He'd pulled up stakes before she could get to know
him—a railroad man with the gypsy in his soul,
apparently. Her mother, a liberated lady before her time,
had never remarried but had raised the child alone, working as a high school teacher in her little town in Pennsylvania. Carolyn had had a boyfriend who had disapproved
of her plan to come to New York to study design and
dressmaking at the Fashion Institute. She had come anyway, graduated and now made a decent living writing
sewing instructions for a pattern company, where she'd
met her friend Sheila, with whom she shared an apartment.

She was twenty-three years old (I'd told her I was
thirty-six and she hadn't blanched visibly). She'd had an
unhappy love affair with a guy who had turned out to be
bad news and I was, she said, her first date in almost a
year. That brought us up to 1963 (the present) by the end
of the veal course.

"And what about you," she asked. "You said last night
you had a three-year-old daughter. Do you have more
family somewhere?"

I told her about my father, and how we both loved
each other but couldn't seem to get past unresolved stuff
from a long time ago. "My grandfather I have fun with,
though. My mother's father. He lives in Vermont and
pops down to visit me. He's 89 and he just hops on the
bus. His second wife died a year ago, and now the old
man is on the loose again. His latest fling was with Mia
Farrow."

"Maureen O'Sullivan's daughter? She's eighteen, isn't

she?"

"That's the one. She hangs out with her mother at the theater. He met her there and he's crazy about her. He was just down here for a week and they were out on the town every night. He'd get home at two in the morning; I'd be pacing around my living room, worrying about him. But of course, he was always fine. 'Oh, we were just out dancing.' He actually toyed with the idea of asking her to marry him. 'If I were only 80 again,' he said. I didn't have the heart to tell him Justice Brandeis had already used the line."

Carolyn laughed delightedly. "Well, you certainly come from hardy stock."

Isador, who had been hovering a few feet away, now approached the table with the suggestion that we top off the meal with steaming cups of Cafe Borgia, a specialty of the house.

"Oh, yes," I said. "It's a magic potion. Whipped cream and grated orange peel and some kind of booze they stir up in the coffee."

The Cafe Borgias came and they *were* magic, causing Carolyn to come home with me that night, and to see me again in a few days, and ultimately to fall in love with me. We courted for two years, both of us knowing we'd wind up together but wary . . . I more than she, I suppose, after what had happened the first time, which had reinforced my general distrust of women.

I took her up to Vermont to meet my grandfather. Actually, she and her friend Sheila and little Michele, who immediately upon meeting Carolyn had become crazy about her, drove up to the tiny town of Hartland, Vermont, on a Saturday in a rented car (since I was still working a six-day week in the play and couldn't get away). Then, on Sunday morning, I hopped a plane and the three females picked me up at the little airport in West Lebanon.

"He tried to sleep with Sheila last night," said Carolyn as we drove back to my grandfather's house. Michele, four years old, smirked in the back seat of the car.

"What?" I turned to Carolyn's friend. "Well, did you sleep with him?"

"I did not," she snapped. "But if you don't watch out, I'll not only sleep with him, I'll *marry* him and get his money and you'll have to call me grandma." (Years later, little Sheila Lukins turned the small catering business she'd started into the multi-million-dollar Silver Palate company and didn't need the money.)

"How the hell did he bring it up?" I asked Carolyn.

"Well, he was showing me through the house and trying to decide where everyone would stay, and I had to tell him that you and I would be sleeping together. 'Oh,' he said, 'I guess things have changed since I was courting Orson's grandmother,' and I didn't know if he was going to be bummed out or what. But he said, 'It's about time, too.' And then he said, 'I wonder if Sheila will sleep with me?' I told him that that would have to be between him and Sheila. Then, she and I got Michele aside and said that no matter *what,* she should say that we three girls were going to have a hen party and sleep in the big bed upstairs . . . and Michele said, 'But I can't do that. Then poor *grandpa* won't have anybody to sleep with.'"

I looked back at Michele, who was just managing to keep from cracking up with laughter.

"So did he ever come right out and ask you, Sheila?"

"He certainly did, Orson. And I told him I was sorry but the answer was no . . . and then, it was so sad. He said to me, 'Oh, I don't *do* anything. It's just that I had a woman in my bed for sixty-three years, and I miss it.'"

Michele crawled up front on to my lap and in a few minutes we were at grandpa's beautiful old Vermont farm house, and I sure was glad to see him. I showed Carolyn the barn where I had used to put on shows in the summer, where Avery Howe, aged ten, who would do anything I told him to (because I was eleven), had climaxed one of my productions with a parachute leap from the top of the barn, holding a massive carriage umbrella, under which he had plummeted to earth like an anvil. I showed her the painting of the Moor girls, one of whom was

President Coolidge's mother, the other my grandfather's.

And for the first time (at Carolyn's urging and with her) I walked to the cemetery where my mother was buried.

"You must have loved her a lot," Carolyn said, and took my hand. I stood there, looking at the gravestone. It had all been so hopeless. How had she got so screwed up? She hadn't known how to love, but could only manipulate and machinate. And of course, that's what I had learned to do, and had spent the rest of my life trying to unlearn. After a while, I answered.

"Yeah, I loved her. I never could get a rise out of her, and it messed me up pretty good, but I'm coming along, and by God I'm happy right now." I looked into Carolyn's eyes. "I love you, sweet woman. Thank you for coming up here, and for suggesting I take a walk over to my mother's grave. I've been resisting doing it for twenty years, and I feel as if a weight has lifted off me." She reached up, took my face in her hands and kissed me.

When grandpa turned ninety, we gave him a party in New York. He had made lots of friends in the city and they turned out en masse for the celebration. Mia Farrow was his date for the evening. Henry Morgan, the comedian, told a joke:

"An old guy of 100 corners a girl of eighteen.

" 'I'm gonna ravish ya,' he tells her, 'and you're gonna yell and scream.' And he ravishes her and she yells and screams.

" 'Now,' he says, 'I'm gonna ravish ya again and you're gonna yell and scream louder.'

"And he ravishes her again and she yells and screams louder.

" 'Now,' he says, 'the next time I ravish ya, you're gonna *sweat.*'

"The girl cowers. 'Why?'

" 'Because,' says the old guy, 'It'll be August!' "

Grandpa roared with laughter. He danced all night. Mia told him about her latest suitor, also an older man. It was the artist, Salvador Dali. Dali, a Spaniard, was an aficianado of the bull ring. Mia detested cruelty to animals, hating needless slaughter. She was even against the concept of zoos. "No one of God's creatures," she said, "should have to live in captivity." Dali decided to test her moral commitment. "I am going to create an original piece of work for you," he told her one day.

A few weeks later, he delivered his present to the Central Park West apartment where Mia lived with her mother. He had hand-blown and painted a vase for her, round at the bottom, long and narrow at the stem. It was breathtakingly beautiful, a priceless Dali original. Inside the vase, fat and contented, was a live mouse. Food could be dropped through the neck of the vase and the mouse could live a long and healthy life as a prisoner. Only by breaking the vase could the mouse be set free. The choice, Dali explained, was Mia's: to preserve a magnificent work of art or to free a common field mouse. The artist himself had no preference, he said; he would find either decision equally interesting. Without a moment's hesitation, Mia carried the vase across the street to Central Park, smashed it on a rock and watched the little gray mouse scamper off into the grass. "Magnificent," cried Dali. "Magificent."

Ninety candles were too many to blow out (and the heat too intense) so everyone helped my grandfather. I was living in an apartment on MacDougal Alley in Greenwich Village. That's where we threw the party and that's where Carolyn and I were married a year later (on October 3rd, 1965). Michele was then five. She'd had mixed feelings when I had first mentioned the idea to her. She was crazy about Carolyn, but not sure she wanted her papa to get married again. When I asked her what she thought, she'd respond with a question of her own: "Who do you love best, me or Carolyn?"

"I love you better as a daughter, and Carolyn better as a girlfriend," I'd answer.

"But which one do you love *best*?" She wouldn't let me off the hook or accept any intellectual distinction.

I talked the problem over with Dr. Baker. He was not

only a therapist, but a man of great wisdom and compassion.

"Tell Michele she's your favorite," was his advice. "She needs that. She's had you all to herself for years and it's hard to give it up."

"But she has to give it up eventually. Won't telling her I love her best make it even harder to do?"

"That's the Freudian idea. But really, what's easier to let go of, something you believe you've wholeheartedly had, or something you've always felt frustrated about?" It suddenly seemed so simple: common sense versus intellectual theory.

The next time the subject of my marrying Carolyn came up, Michele asked her question once again. I looked around conspiratorially, then whispered, "Let's not tell Carolyn . . . we don't want to hurt her feelings . . . but I love you best." Her face lit up like a shooting star.

"You do? Honest?"

"Yeah."

She laughed delightedly. Then she said, "I won't tell her. And I guess it's OK if you marry her. Do I get to be flower girl?"

It was a big wedding. Grandpa came back down from Vermont, and we were very much in love. A year later our son Max was born. We named him for Maurice Sendak's Max in *Where the Wild Things Are*. Sendak, a friend, drew a birth announcement for us. It showed his Max, in wolf suit, nailing up a poster about the new baby.

We were living in my apartment and had to cram the new arrival into a small dressing area off the master bedroom. "A family needs a home," said Carolyn. "If we're going to stay in New York, do you think we could afford to buy a house?" Sure we could. Money was never a problem with us. In the nineteen sixties, I starred in one Broadway show after another. At the same time, I was appearing five times a week on *To Tell the Truth* as well as on Johnny Carson's show (frequently as substitute host) and Merv Griffin's. I also did the voices for commercials.

Carolyn found a realtor in the Yellow Pages, who hustled her off on a tour of Manhattan. When she had made her selection, she urged me to come see it. I was appalled. The place she had chosen was an ancient wreck in a working class no man's land between the Village and Chelsea, on 15th Street. Though it still had faint vestiges of former glory, its most recent incarnation had been as a rooming house. The roof was caved in and the floors were spongy from decades of water damage. Countless partitions had been erected, and inept and illegal plumbing had been installed for a warren of tiny rooms. Everything in the house was coming apart.

"God, honey," I said. "We'll have to replace the roof, the floors, the walls and most of the supporting beams. The place looks like it's being held up by memory."

Carolyn's face was glowing. "We checked the records at City Hall, and the first deed to this house was recorded on October 3rd, 1865. One hundred years to the day. It's a sign. Oh, I do love it, Orson, I want it."

I stood there in the mouldering ruin and shook my head in wonder. She could have chosen a much fancier place. Instead, she had looked at this pile of debris and seen a miracle. We bought the house and set about restoring it. Carolyn acted as general contractor, drawing up plans with an architect, then hiring builders and supervising the work. "If you want things done right, you have to be there all the time anyway," she said.

We found an eccentric Puerto Rican carpenter named Perez to do the job. Louie Rosenthal, a three-hundred-pound plumber installed the pipes. He and his van were covered with grease at all times. He loved his work more than anyone I've ever known. "Look at this," he'd say, fondling a length of copper pipe, Michelangelo selecting marble. "It's beautiful. It cries out to be threaded."

Perez was a superb carpenter. He was determined to restore the house to its original glory. He fashioned decorative molding out of wood to replace the gutted plaster molding. Like many artists, he was difficult to work with. He enjoyed having no general contractor to

dictate to him and was pleased to be dealing directly with
Carolyn. He was a perfectionist and moved ahead slowly.

We put up with his eccentricities and he put up with
ours. Ever since I was a little boy, growing up on movies
like *Frankenstein* and *Dracula,* I had fantasized about
some day owning a house with a secret passage in it.
Perez thought I was crazy. But he constructed my secret
passage for me. Its entrance was hidden behind a built-in
wall mirror. A narrow corridor then snaked along and
re-emerged behind a similar mirror in another room. I
was as happy as a hunchback.

Carolyn supervised all the work. She learned the
lumber yards and supply houses, traveling all over
Manhattan and Queens to order doors or select hardware
and fixtures. Money was no object; we wanted a showplace. The house was four stories high and we had a
working fireplace in every major room. Perez would complete a room and call us over to admire his finishing
touches. "Look at this molding I've made," he'd say,
pointing to the ceiling. "Plasterers in Spain spend years
learning to make molding like that."

The renovation progressed slowly. Perez would scream
that he couldn't work with the electrician, or that
Rosenthal the plumber hadn't installed the toilets on time.
We were desperate to move into the house.

In the midst of all this, I received an offer to appear
opposite Melina Mercouri in a show called *Illya Darling,*
a musical stage version of her film *Never on Sunday.* This
was my biggest break yet. There was enormous excitement surrounding the show. It had a huge advance sale.
Melina's husband, Jules Dassin, had written it and was
directing, based on his work for the film. I'd be playing
the part he'd played in his own picture, the idealistic
American who falls in love with Melina and with Greece.

Melina was stunningly beautiful, and the most dynamic
human being I've ever met. She gave new meaning to the
phrase "larger than life." Her ego was colossal, yet there
was no hint of meanness in her. On a lunch break during
rehearsals one day, she was interviewed by *The New York*

Times. As she talked to the reporter, her secretary fed her . . . actually cut her steak and potatoes into small pieces and placed them into her mouth on the end of a fork. This was because Melina needed her hands to talk with. It made absolute sense . . . and I couldn't think of anyone else in the world who would have done it, with the possible exception of Kind Saud.

The show opened to less than ecstatic reviews. It didn't matter. Everyone on both sides of the footlights loved Melina and she packed them in. A few months later, word came that Athens had fallen to a military coup; the government of Greece would become fascist. Gloom spread over the Greek members of the company. Melina wailed in her dressing room.

"Oh, God," she cried. "Oh, God. First the critics hate the show, then the father of a friend of mine dies and now this. What will they do to me next?"

The renovations on our house were finally completed and the place was a marvel. On the second story was a ballroom with floor-to-ceiling French doors which looked out onto the street in front and onto our garden in the back. The garden was professionally designed and planted. On the ground floor, a huge kitchen-family room gave onto the yard. A formal dining room faced the street. The master bedroom was on the third floor and up top was kiddie land. Soon it would be filled; Carolyn was expecting again.

When she was in her eighth month, we saw that our pet cat was pregnant, too. The cat's time came and she sought out her mistress, meowing and running back and forth. Carolyn followed her to the closet of the nursery we'd prepared for our coming baby. There, the cat had chosen to make her nest. She clearly wanted the company of another female. Lying on an old towel we spread out for her, she panted rythmically, looking into Carolyn's eyes.

We were enrolled at that time in a Lamaze class, where husbands learned to coach their wives in breathing techniques. I walked into the nursery and crouched next to where Carolyn sat whispering words of encouragement to the laboring cat. We were fascinated by her breathing; a series of fast pants, followed by long, slow breaths, then the quick panting again.

"It's exactly what we're studying in Lamaze class," said Carolyn. And she was right; the rhythm was identical.

Later, after our daughter Susannah had been born and had moved into that little nursery, she developed, at the age of ten days, a severe case of flu (which was rampant in the city) and a dangerously high fever.

"There's nothing we can do to treat her," said the anxious doctor. "It's almost unheard of for infants of this age to contract respiratory infections. I'm afraid I can't offer you a lot of hope. Turn on a humidifier to help her breathe, stay with her, and pray. There's nothing else we can do for the poor little thing."

And stay with her Carolyn did. For five days she lived in the little room, hardly sleeping, holding her child, breast-feeding her when she agreed to nurse, gazing at her, crooning softly to her, filling the poor, sick baby with love. The humidifier ran until the new wallpaper peeled off the nursery walls. On the fifth day, the fever broke and we knew that Susie was going to live. Then Carolyn came out, collapsed in her bed and slept.

"It was love saved that little girl," said the doctor. "Only love."

With a house that large, we needed a sizeable staff. Bridie had moved back to Ireland (after staying with Michele for five years) and a succession of English nannies came to live with us, to help look after the children. Tellervo, our Finnish housekeeper, came five days a week, and a Black guy named Warren did the heavy cleaning on Tuesdays and Fridays. He also acted as butler occasionally when we gave dinner parties. I had an art collection and there were paintings on every wall.

Illya Darling settled in for a healthy run at the Mark Hellinger Theater on Broadway. At the same time, I continued to appear on *To Tell the Truth* every day, as well as on all the TV talk shows. The money was pouring in. A lot of it poured back out, too. I had read a book called *Summerhill* about a school in England based on principles of self-government. There wasn't a school like it in America and Michele was due to enter first grade soon. I decided to put down $35,000 on a building, advertise for teachers and open an American Summerhill school. The enterprise was a success. Running it was a full-time job, which I performed (with Carolyn's help) in addition to all my other work. (My book, *Me and the Orgone*, published by St. Martin's Press in 1971, tells about the school and my experience in Reichian therapy. It's still in print.)

We settled into our new house, loving it. Outside, the sixties rolled by. Summer weekends we spent at a little beach house I had built in Westhampton. Once or twice a year we gave huge parties, mainly so we could use the ballroom. A hundred guests would come. They'd wander through the house, exploring it, carrying their glasses of wine. There were famous celebrities and just average people whom we knew and liked. If the neighbors called the cops about the noise, we'd invite the cops to the party. Then we'd ask the neighbors in, too.

One of our friends was a beautiful young woman named Marina Romanov. She was one of *the* Romanovs and a princess. When she got married, White Russians came from all over the country to attend the ceremony. After the wedding, Marina invited us to a dinner party at her place in the East 70s. It was a large, rent-controlled apartment in an old building. White Russians have style but not much money.

On the night of the party, cocktails were served in the living room and there were heated discussions about Vietnam. It was 1968. Most of the White Russians were hawks. A few of the younger ones were against the war. An old family retainer padded around serving Gallo chablis from an antique decanter. I took a great liking to a guy named Arkady Nebelsine. He came from a famous old Russian family and had a fine sense of humor. I took a dislike to an angry young woman who seemed to be doing a number on her husband. The couple looked like society types. Whatever he said, she'd ridicule.

We moved into the dining room to eat. Carolyn was seated way down on the opposite side of the table from me. Nebelsine was at the far end, and Marina was at the head of the table. The society bitch was across from me. The old retainer and another servant brought food out and ran around filling wine glasses from the decanter. After dinner, there was champagne and it was time for the Old Russian custom of toasting. By tradition, all twenty-four diners would have to propose toasts.

The first guest stood up and toasted Marina and her new husband, Bill Beadleston. We all drank their health. The next person hoped the new couple would produce lots of children and we drank to that. Several variations on wedding and marriage themes followed. Then someone suggested that we drink to the memory of the Czar. I toyed with the idea of toasting Rasputin but decided it would be in bad taste.

Then it was the society bitch's turn. She'd been into the wine at some length by that time and was disagreeably sloshed. She stood up, raised her glass, fixed an eye on her poor husband down the way and said, "To Jack. Last night was our first wedding anniversary. I wore my wedding night nightgown, but a fat lot of good it did. Well, here's to the next fifty years, or however the hell long it has to be." She sat down.

Carolyn and I sneaked a look at each other. She seemed as appalled as I was. To my disgust, the reaction in the room was neither outrage nor shock. People tittered as if something amusing had been said. Manners apparently required that the woman's hostility not be noticed, or offense taken. It was my turn to toast next. I stood up, raised my champagne glass and said, "To my wife. The best fuck I've ever had."

There was an awful silence and then Arkady Nebelsine

let out a whoop of delight. That broke the ice and some of the other people began to laugh, too. But most of the guest stared down at their plates. The society bitch got back up and raised her glass again.

"To Mrs. Bean," she said, "for having the courage to live with this man."

"Hear, hear," said a voice from somewhere at the table.

Carolyn looked stunningly beautiful that night. She rose gracefully, lifted her glass and said, "To my husband. The best fuck *I've* ever had." Arkady Nebelsine fell off his chair. His laughter shook the table. About a third of the group howled as well, but the rest were appalled. Two people stood up and walked out of the room. Poor Marina didn't know what had hit her.

I was on a roll and couldn't quit when I was ahead. A terrible, self-destructive urge took me over. I stood up again and raised my glass to my main supporter at the table. "To Arkady Nebelsine," I said, "whose grandfather buggered a moose in the Pokrov Woods." The laugh froze on Nebelsine's lips.

"Now you've gone too far," he said.

"Your grandfather buggers a moose and *I've* gone too far?" There was pandemonium at the table. Arkady Nebelsine began to laugh again, joined by his friends. Other people got up to leave. The old servant desperately poured champagne. I expected Bill Beadleston to come over and slug me. I finally shut up and the evening ran its course.

We never saw any of the people at the party again. I sent flowers to Marina the next day, and a note of apology. But actually I thought the whole thing had been wonderful. Sydney would have been proud of me. And God how I loved Carolyn for coming to my defense.

Years of political mismanagement had finally caught up and New York was teetering on the brink of bankruptcy. Sirens screamed in the night and the city was coming apart. Every day the newspapers predicted financial collapse. Garbage was picked up intermittently, the subway system became a disaster, the crime rate rose, dog shit was everywhere and teachers, cops and firemen were threatening walkouts.

The house we'd built became our refuge of tranquility. On one side of us lived an elderly widow. On the other side was a large building run by the Catholic Church as a retreat for an order of nuns. There was a big tree in our back yard and on summer evenings we'd sit under it and listen to the tinkling of the bells that called the nuns to prayer. When I was in my house, the world outside seemed far away.

Grandpa came down to New York to spend Christmas with us and see the new house. He was ninety-three. On Christmas Eve, Carolyn had an idea.

"Let's ask the nuns from next door if they want to come over," she said.

I knew the Mother Superior; she was a fan of mine from *To Tell the Truth*. When I asked her, she thought for a moment and then said, "Why not? I'll bring the girls over after vespers. There are a dozen of us. Will that be alright?"

I asked if it was proper to offer the sisters a drink.

"Sure," said the Mother Superior. "It's Christmas Eve and our blessed Savior never objected to a little taste."

The girls showed up in about an hour. They *were* girls, most of them: young novitiates. They ooed and aahed around the house, then sat down in our formal parlor, off the ballroom. I brought out a tray of liqueurs, green Creme de Menthe, golden Galiano, and a purple beverage called Parfait Amour. Everyone had a taste of each color, and then another taste. We sang Christmas carols. Grandpa sat next to the Mother Superior, holding her hand and making her laugh. We all got pleasantly tipsy. The children ran in and out of the room excitedly. Grandpa put his arm around the Mother Superior.

"You're a damn good-looking woman," he told her. "Even if you are a nun."

The sisters went back to their convent happy.

Without meaning to, we'd caused some trouble in our neighborhood. The block we were on was a poor one, filled with working class families. Syrians, Turks, Puerto Ricans and Blacks lived there. At first, we were a welcome diversion for them. "Hey Orson, get me on television," they'd yell. But the fancy place we'd built upgraded the block. Speculators began buying houses and evicting tenants. People started to resent us.

The widow next door sold her house and moved away. The speculator who bought the place let it sit empty while he waited for the price to go up. The Catholic Church decided to close its retreat and moved the nuns to Staten Island. It rented the building to Daytop Village, a halfway house for former drug addicts. The block was going schizoid.

Kids from the neighborhood smashed the windows of the house the old lady had vacated. Thieves broke into it and carried away the copper pipes, the marble from the fireplaces and anything else they could find that was worth money. Then junkies moved in and squatted there, lighting fires to sterilize their needles, and sleeping off their fixes on piles of debris. Every night when we went to bed we could hear them walking around next door. We wondered when one of them would drop a match and set fire to the house. Once in a while, we'd call the cops and they'd come and chase the junkies away, but the next day they'd be back.

A hundred ex-addicts came to live at Daytop Village. The noise level on the block rose substantially. One night, we woke up hearing screams. "No, no," cried a terrified voice. "Don't. Please help me." It sounded like murder. We called the local precinct house and they sent a squad car. I pulled a pair of pants on over my pajamas and met the cops in the street. The screams sounded like they were coming from the empty house next door, but they weren't. The boys in Daytop had decided to work out their fears and aggressions in an impromptu encounter session.

On another night, Carolyn shook me awake. "There's

something going on down at the front door," she said. I couldn't hear anything but to appease her, I put on my bathrobe and tiptoed down the stairs. As I approached the door, I heard the sound too. I came close, then yelled as loud as I could: "Get the hell out of here!" I heard a frantic scuffling, then footsteps retreating down the street. I opened the door in time to see a shadowy figure disappearing into the night. The door had a sizable hole gouged out of it, next to the lock. The realization that we were not safe in our castle was a chilling one. We had the house wired by a security company and started checking doors and windows every night.

Life was coming unravelled for me. I was trying to cram too much into it. I taped my TV programs in the morning, did my stage shows at night and ran the school in between. I seldom got enough sleep and rarely found time to spend with the children. When I was home, Carolyn would shoo them out of the room saying, "Shh. Daddy's tired."

America seemed to feel the way I did: it was being torn apart. I brooded about my country. What we were doing in Vietnam was poisoning us at home. The Kent State massacre had taken place and there were confrontations every day in the streets of New York. Then one afternoon, I heard a big explosion and the Spode china in our dining room cabinet shook. Following the sound of sirens, I walked over to 11th Street. There was a hulking wreck where a house had once been. It turned out the Students for a Democratic Society had been using the place as a bomb factory.

The neighborhood was well-to-do-liberal Greenwich Village and one of the people from the block was standing in front of the wreckage, talking to a friend. "Those kids were protesting inequities in the system," she said. Madness. It seemed to me the city was going crazy. The country too. And I felt that if I didn't do something soon to make a change in my life, I was going to join them.

I picked my way home along the sidewalk. Carolyn was in the kitchen helping Tellervo polish the silver. "Come on out back," I said to her. Leaving her jar of Gorham's on the butcher-block table, she followed me into the yard. I positioned a couple of our outdoor chairs and motioned that she should sit down. Then I sat down beside her.

"The house next to Dusty's place on 11th Street is gone," I said. (Dustin Hoffman was a friend. We'd worked together in a Maxwell Anderson play, *The Starwagon*.)

"What do you mean?"

"I mean that somebody has blown the fucking thing up. It's gone. There's nothing there." It took a moment for the information to sink in.

"Who did it?"

"Some kids from the Weather Underground, apparently. A couple of them were blown to bits by their own bombs."

We sat in the yard and talked for an hour. I told her about the fears that had been churning around in my mind: that America was going to go fascist . . . that the push from the left was so strong that the generals were going to take over. Pumping up my wind box, I gave her a history lesson about the Jews in Germany: the smartest ones had gotten out with what they owned, the next smartest ones had gotten out with their lives, and most of them had just stayed put till it was too late, saying "It can't happen here." She sat listening to me, holding on to the arms of her chair. A trio of starlings landed in the garden behind us and walked around looking for something to eat. Inside, Tellervo cleaned the kitchen.

A plan had been simmering in my mind for the past few months. Suddenly it came to a boil. I leaned forward and took hold of Carolyn's hand. "Let's have an adventure," I said. "Let's sell the house, get the hell out of here and move to Australia." She stared at me dumbstruck. "Well, why not? They speak English down there, sort of. I'm sure I'll be able to get work on Aussie TV. The climate's supposed to be great and it would be an incredible experience for the kids."

"But our beautiful house," she whispered. "And what

about your career? And our friends and my mother and the school. And Max just got started in his new play group."

There was really nothing to hold us here, I explained. Or to hold us anywhere, for that matter. I'd always be able to make a living one way or another *wherever* we were. And anyhow, we had plenty of dough stashed away. Sure, the house was great but we could build another one just as great somewhere. Stuff can own people, if they don't watch out: grass demanding to be cut, silver demanding to be polished. I told her I'd been feeling lately as if I were working for Tellervo and Warren and all the nannies, instead of their working for me.

"The country is turning to gorilla shit," I wailed. "So is New York and so are we. I'm too tired to make love to you, my kids are growing up without me, and what do we need with all this money I'm earning if it doesn't buy us what we want?"

Carolyn sat, taking it in. Then she smiled, shrugged her shoulders and said, "OK, let's go."

I stared at her in disbelief. I had another three-quarters of an hour of persuasion ready. "Do you mean it? Really? It's alright?"

"Why not? We can always come back if we don't like Australia." I stood up and pulled her to me.

"God, I love you," I said. "You're the best wife any man ever had. You're Superwife." (And she was. But nothing comes for free, and she was starting to pay a price for being perfect.)

We decided to go Down Under for a year and check it out. Then we'd make up our minds about whether to stay for a second year or not. We talked over our plan with the kids. Michele was the only one it would really affect. She'd been flying over to Europe every summer to spend time with her mother.

"But Australia has summer in the winter, so how will I be able to go to France?" she asked.

"The schools have a long midwinter vacation in July

and August," I told her. Carolyn had called the consulate and done some checking. "You'll be able to tell your mom and stepbrothers all about kangaroos."

"OK, Papa. Whatever you say."

We turned the school over to the teachers. It was a non-profit educational foundation. I had poured a hundred thousand dollars into it. It lasted for a total of sixteen years and the waves it made in the world of education are still rippling.

Friends and relations reacted to the news of our upcoming departure in different ways. Grandpa said he'd always wanted to visit Australia and that this would be a good excuse. Carolyn's mother was great. My agent wept real tears. People reacted with grudging admiration or sometimes with anger.

"If you don't like what's happening to the country, you should stay and fight to change it," our liberal friends would crab. The more conservative ones looked wistful. "I wish I were in a position to do something like that." I don't know what position they thought I was in. But I had something they didn't have. I was crazy. I also had a wife who'd go anywhere with me.

We put the house on the market and asked a fortune for it. Who the hell is going to buy a showplace on a run-down block full of Turks and Syrians, I wondered? One day the realtor brought an eccentric rich lady to see the house. She had a ten-year-old kid on whom she obviously doted. Carolyn showed her around while the boy watched our TV.

"Psst. Hey kid, you wanna see something?" I took him in the other room, slid the wall mirror back and there was the secret passage. His eyes were like frisbees. He stepped inside and when he came out the other end he whispered, "Oh wow." Then he ran out of the room calling, "Mom, hey Mom!" I knew we'd made a sale.

I had it figured out in my mind that the generals' coup would take place on July 4th, a symbolic date. So we booked passage to Sydney on the 3rd. At the last minute we were invited to a swell 4th of July party, so we changed the reservations to the 5th. That's how crazy we were.

We shipped a few pieces of furniture and most of our paintings to Australia. The rest of our stuff we got rid of in a giant yard sale or gave to the Salvation Army. I didn't care about our beautiful house any more. I had put it behind me. Whatever Carolyn felt, she kept to herself. It was in her nature to plunge wholeheartedly into whatever she decided to do. She would follow where I led.

An Australian theatrical company came to New York looking for a star for the Aussie version of the hit Broadway musical, *Promises, Promises.* I applied for and was given the part. The show would open in Melbourne and then play Sydney. What a wonderful introduction to the country. I'd be a big frog in a little puddle. Not bad.

The trip to Australia took twenty hours flying time. It was 1970. Michele was eleven, Max was four and little Susie was two.

Off we flew, waving goodbye to America, perhaps forever. What an upheaval . . . what drama . . . how I loved it.

VI

I wake up after a bad dream, sweating and anxious.
Desperately, I try to remember the dream: something
about a group of agents passing judgment on me, a variation on the actor's nightmare. Frightened, angry, my
muscles aching, I crawl out of bed: "Jesus, I'm 58 years
old. Will I always be at the mercy of my damned
dreams?" I try to recall the dream, the way I used to do
when I was in analysis, hoping to understand it and
diminish my anxiety. It's no use. I can't remember. I'm
screwed. Now I'll be bummed out for the day . . . a victim of my lousy ego, even when I'm asleep.

"Wait a minute. My ego. That guy's the enemy. My
ego's not me. Remember, schmuck? He just wants to be
in charge at all costs, and is more than happy to shaft the
Orson organization in the process. He's the Great
Deceiver. He slips the dream in when I'm not looking,
then whispers. 'Look how shitty you feel. You've got a
problem to solve. Here, let me help you.' I get involved in
solutions (his game); I'm distracted from just being happy
(from just *being*)."

79

I pull on my beat-up old bathrobe and shuffle into the kitchen to brew my morning coffee. "The wily bastard. I can't win, playing his game. If I do find a solution, he'll just slip in another problem. Why the hell am I falling for his tricks again?" I start to grin. I'm seeing that I can simply decide my anxious feelings aren't a problem. As I begin to believe that, the feelings are fading. The dream brought them to me; the dream is past; the feelings are past. Now is now. I'm not having the dream now; the feelings are fading now. Now is the only time there is. Now is full of love and healing.

The anxiety is simply drifting away. I sit down to drink my Taster's Choice. I think about a TV interview I once saw, I believe on *60 Minutes,* with the real-life heroine of the made-for-TV-movie *Playing for Time.* The tall, gaunt and morose Vanessa Redgrave had starred as the French woman who survived the Nazi concentration camps by playing in the orchestra that provided the music by which her fellow inmates marched to the gas chamber. The show had been powerful and predictably depressing.

The real-life heroine had turned out to be short, roly-poly and delightfully upbeat. When the interviewer had asked if she were bitter about her experiences, she had answered (words to the effect of), "Oh no. That's all in the past. The sun is out today and I'm living in La Belle Paree. I won't let them [the Nazis] have me now. The only time they get to me is in my dreams. Every morning I wake up terrified. Then, I get out of bed, shake myself and say, 'Enough of that.' Then I feel fine." She had laughed delightedly and, watching at home, I had laughed with her.

Venice, California, 1987

VII

We were back on a block with Turks and Syrians. Australia was in the midst of its "Populate or Perish" campaign. The country was experiencing a full-employment boom and needed people for the jobs Aussies refused to do: street cleaner, garbage man, and the like. Immigrants (mostly Mediterranean types) were lured with free passage and a guarantee of work.

We were living in Melbourne, the more conservative of Australia's two major cities. The pubs closed at ten P.M. and after that, if you wanted a beer, you drank at home. The neighborhood we were in, not far from "downtown" where my show was rehearsing, had become a European melting pot. There were little Mulberry Street-type shops filled with Italian cheese, Syrian bread and signs in a dozen different languages.

Michele was enrolled in sixth grade at the local public school. I bragged to one of the Australian actors in the show that she'd won first prize in a foot race. "Christ," he said. "There's nothing but wops and Greeks in that school. She didn't win over any real Aussies." He was kidding on the square.

We had rented a small, furnished, two story "terrace house" on a tree lined street. It had no central heat; practically no Aussie lived with such a luxury. And by building code, there were ventilator holes through the exterior wall of each room, leading to the outside air: ("A house has to breathe, mate.") The Bean family froze. I mean, it *was* July (things warmed up by October). There was a fireplace in the living room. We called Farnsworth for Firewood and laid in a supply of Mallee roots. These were the gnarled, long-burning roots of the Mallee tree (or something like that). It was necessary to construct a regular fire first; then, when it was blazing, a Mallee root placed on top of it would slowly catch and burn for the rest of the day.

Getting out of bed in the morning was hard. We slept upstairs, huddled under layers of blankets. Dad got up first, to build a fire. It seemed like man's work to me and Carolyn was happy to accede to the sexist thinking. When the chill was off the room, I'd yell upstairs and the rest of the crew would tumble down, the children running to the fireplace, Carolyn going into the kitchen to prepare breakfast. Aussie friends made fun of us. "You Americans are too soft," they'd snort. They were right. When we finally adjusted to the cooler temperature, we never went back to our old ways and have felt overheated in America ever since.

The milkman's horse clopped by at four o'clock every morning and the milk was delivered in pint bottles, English style. There were no paper bags in the little store on the corner; we learned to bring a cloth sack from home. Eggs were individually wrapped in pieces of newspaper. Life ran at a slower pace than it had in New York.

One day, I took a cab home from rehearsal and then realized I'd left my script in it. "Oh God," I moaned. Fifteen minutes later, there was a knock on the door. "G'day, mate." The cab driver had found the script, remembered where he'd dropped me off and had come to return it. And no tip accepted. Australia charmed us.

Promises, Promises was scheduled to play a few months in Melbourne and then move on to Sydney. That's where we knew we wanted to live. Sydney was Australia's big apple. Carolyn's description of it: "If London and New York had a baby." When rehearsals were over and the show had opened (to fairly unenthusiastic reviews), we started taking the one-hour shuttle flight to Sydney on my day off each week, looking for a house to buy. On the second try, we found one. The realtor, a man named Fred Weston, had shown us most of what was available. Suddenly, he snapped his fingers as if a thought had just occurred to him.

"There is one house . . ." He paused.

"Yes?"

"Oh, I don't know if you'd be interested."

"Well, show it to us."

Dark and forbidding, the house squatted on a hill overlooking Sydney harbor. Overlooking it completely, I should have said. There were no windows on the harbor side. The house had been set down middle class proper, facing the road, ignoring what was out back. A storage room and a laundry faced one of the great scenic waterways in the world. What windows there were, in the front, were all boarded up. The place had been built in the Twenties and owned, we subsequently found out, by a Hungarian doctor who had died in it.

"Look at this," said Carolyn as we walked through the deserted house. On both sides of every interior door there were at least three and sometimes as many as four slide bolt locks. Every room in the house could be locked off from every other room. "What the hell was going on in here, devil worship?"

But the price was right and Carolyn, applying her dressmaker's eye, could see the potential. "We'll turn the place around," she said. "Their old parlor will be our bedroom. Wouldn't it be nice to have a bedroom with a fireplace again? We'll knock down these walls and open everything up. We'll put in big French doors facing the harbor and this whole area will be our living room. Then we'll add a deck to sit on and watch the sun go down over the water."

"We'll take it," I told Fred Weston. We'd made friends with a Melbourne architect who found us a man in Sydney to draw up Carolyn's plans. And he in turn found us the Davison brothers.

"Jack does the building and I handle the business end of things," said Mr. William Davison, a portly gent in his mid-fifties. As far as I could see, that meant we were paying two men to do the job of one. But we were desperate to move into the house when the show shifted from Melbourne to Sydney.

"Don't worry," said William Davison. "We'll have you and the little ones in here, snug as koalas in gum trees." The little ones would include another, we'd found out. We were going to have our very one 'roo, conceived on a Sunday in Melbourne, when there's not a pub in town open, and not much other reason to leave the house.

Koalas would have given up gum trees if they were no more snug than we were when we finally made the move to Sydney. Two rooms was what we had, for five and a half of us, while the work went on in the rest of the house. On it went, and on and on . . . and plaster dust became our second skin. The Davison brothers and their plumbers, electricians and helpers worked on the place for weeks on end, moving at a pace an American snail would have sneered at. They (and Aussies in general) seemed to have no concept of efficiency as Americans think of it.

I came across the electrician one day running cable from an on-off switch on the wall to an overhead light in our bedroom closet.

"Why don't you just install one of those porcelain ceiling fixtures with a string pull on it?" I asked him. "That would cost you a fraction of what this elaborate set-up will. I mean after all, it's only a closet."

"What are you talking about, Mr. Bean?" He'd never heard of such a device. I made a drawing for him of the fixture, which could be purchased in any American hardware store for $3.95. "Why, that's marvelous," he exclaimed, shaking his head in wonder. "An invention like this would be worth a lot." Then he handed the paper back to me, turned away and resumed the installation of his cable.

On another day, I found brother Jack Davison sitting in front of a pile of bricks he'd saved from one of our demolished walls. He was carefully chipping the old, used mortar off each brick. I asked him why he was doing it.

"These bricks are perfectly good, mate. We can use them under the new back porch."

"But I'm paying you ten bucks an hour, Jack. We can toss these bricks out and buy new ones for a third of what it'll cost to save them."

He looked at me thoughtfully for a moment, then said: "You can't throw away perfectly good brick, mate."

"But it's costing us a fortune to save it."

He reached into his pocket, pulled out an old blue bandana and began polishing the blade of his chisel. Then he smiled pleasantly at me. "You can't throw away perfectly good brick." An invisible curtain lowered between us, and I could see there was no point in going on with the discussion.

"That's the way we do it down here." Again and again, I heard that refrain in Australia. An American business man we befriended in a restaurant (the minute we heard Stateside accents, we started talking to strangers) told us that Pepsi-Cola of America had sent him to Sydney to find out why the Aussie subsidiary had not increased its share of the market in fifteen years. He said he'd found inefficient bottling and distributing techniques and outdated ad campaigns. He gave his Aussie hosts the benefit of his good old American know-how. "Systems like this went out twenty years ago," he told them.

They smiled at him pleasantly. "That's the way we do it down here," they said.

"But you could increase your productivity by twenty percent with almost no additional expense."

"You don't understand, mate. That's the way we do it

down here." The conversation was clearly closed. Then, the good men of Pepsi-Cola Australia clapped their American visitor on the back. "Let's go for a sail on the harbor," they said.

A sail on the harbor. It was what Sydneysiders seemed to live for.

At Double Bay Dry Cleaners, I asked the proprietor if my pants could be ready by Saturday.

"Sorry, mate. We're closed on Saturdays. That's when I go sailing on the harbor.

At Vaucluse Ford Auto Repair: "Do you think I can pick up the car late Friday, please?"

"Sorry, mate. We close early on Fridays. I take my boy sailing on the harbor."

Intellectually I could see the benefits; emotionally, I was still an American.

One day, Mr. William Davison brought us a large fish he'd caught and a bottle of Australian champagne. "To celebrate the completion of the job, mate," he said, and proudly popped open the bottle. I looked around at the mess we were living with.

"But it's nowhere near complete," I said.

"Wrong, mate. That's your non-professional's eye view of things. The construction is done. What's left is only cosmetic finishing touches." Weeks more dragged on while such cosmetic touches as 2 × 4's and brick retaining walls were added to the house. Finally the work was over, the Davisons left and the last of the plaster dust was vacuumed out of the rugs. Our stuff had arrived from New York and now Carolyn hung pictures and shoved furniture around. We bought new things, too.

"Everything in Sydney is from two seasons ago in the States," Carolyn complained. But when the house was done, it was a showplace to rival 15th Street: a Mediterranean villa filled with windows and painted a dazzling high-gloss white. Casablanca fans hung from the ceiling and eight-foot French doors led to a huge deck overlooking the harbor. And what a view it was . . . sailboats and ocean liners passed one another on the finest natural harbor in the world right before our eyes.

In the distance, off to the left, just out of sight around the bend, was the Sydney Opera House. In the foreground, sunning himself on a rock next to a tiny natural waterfall was our very own water lizard, a two-foot-long, prehistoric-looking iguana (Aussies call them goannas). He'd lived in the neighborhood for years, apparently, and was quite tame, coming to the porch to catch scraps of food the kids would throw to him, and even occasionally allowing himself to be petted. We also had a possum who lived in our attic. We saw him infrequently but could hear him walking around above us at night.

"It's cozy to have him up there," said Carolyn. "Nicer than the junkies we used to hear in New York."

Our property fronted on a preserve that ran all the way down to Parsley Bay, part of over 300 miles of waterfront within the city limits of Sydney. The yard between the house and the road was overflowing with palm trees, jacaranda trees, eucalyptus (gum) trees and a riot of flowers: white, pink, red and yellow roses, zinnias and gardenias.

Through a neighbor, we found Giovanni, an Italian-Australian immigrant gardener who came three days a week to look after our yard. "Giovanni likes a cold can, Mrs. Bean," he told the lady of the house. "I'll just come in the kitchen and help myself . . . you won't have to be bothered." A six-pack a day of Foster's Lager was what Giovanni liked, but he kept the grounds looking trim. We also hired a live-in baby sitter, a young English emigrée named Louise.

We could walk down to Parsley Bay for a dip in the harbor behind the shark net (shudder), or we could drive ten minutes to Bondi Beach, the world-class surfer's paradise smack in the city. There, the shark problem was handled by combination lifeguard/shark watch boys, who sat on high towers every hundred yards or so along the beach. When they honked their warning horns, you can believe the surf emptied out fast.

"There's nothing to be alarmed about, mate," a fellow

bather said to me one day. "We haven't had a fatal shark attack here at Bondi in twenty years." I blanched at the thought of what a *non*-fatal shark attack might leave hobbling around.

But we did grow braver in time. Some people we met, who owned a beautiful power launch, invited us for a day of cruising the inner reaches of Sydney Harbor. In secluded little coves, we anchored and dove off the end of the boat. We didn't stay in the water for long. It was in just such a cove that the late Prime Minister Holt had gone for a morning swim and never been heard from again. Sharks like the warmth of shallow coves, where inland streams empty into the harbor.

The "bird watching" on the beach was incredible. The bikinis were like Band-Aids, quite startling for 1970 (now I hear the Sydney beaches are topless), and the bodies of both sexes spectacular, since all Aussies live on the tennis court from the age of six months.

My stage show, *Promises, Promises*, with its hip American humor and off-beat musical arrangements, was enjoying only limited success with the Aussies. Sophisticated theatergoers were few and far between. The country is not the new frontier Americans think it is. Australia is a remnant of the British Empire, where people who couldn't make it in India were sent.

November rolled around (it was starting to get hot) and for the first time we began to get homesick, when we looked at the calendar and realized it would soon be Thanksgiving back in the states. Sydney was an R and R center for our boys in Vietnam. They'd fly there for a week's respite from the war. We called the local USO headquarters and said, "Send us a dozen G.I.s for an American Thanksgiving." The boys were invited to come at noon for swimming, followed by dinner.

There were a lot of good-looking girls in *Promises, Promises*. I asked twelve of them to be the soldiers' dates. When the G.I.s showed up, they found beautiful young women in bikinis waiting to take them down to Parsley

Bay. In the late afternoon we had turkey, and that night, compliments of the management, there were free seats for all at the show. At least one romance blossomed out of that Thanksgiving. A Marine named Kelly flew back from Saigon to see one of the dancers. It really is more blessed to give than to receive. It was the best Thanksgiving we ever had.

Life in Australia was very different from what it had been for me back home. I could walk on the streets of Sydney without being spotted by a living soul. The unfamiliarity of it made me nervous. Part of me liked being anonymous; part of me didn't. Realistically, the only genuine benefit to celebrity status is being recognized by headwaiters and given good tables in restaurants. The rest of it is part ego trip, part inconvenience. Anyway, I had always chosen to keep my notoriety within limits, walking the thin line between fame and oblivion.

My energy was very high. I was in a continuous state of arousal, and would happily have wrestled Carolyn into bed three times a day. But unfortunately for me she seemed to have put her passion on hold since arriving in Australia. We talked about it, when I insisted on doing so, and the explanation she came up with was that when she had denied the anxiety she had felt at leaving home, friends and mother, the rest of her feelings had willy-nilly shut down, too.

"Be patient with me," she pleaded. I tried, but it wasn't easy.

When the show finally closed (after an OK run of six months), I had more time to contemplate life, Sydney Harbor and my navel. An old Chinese proverb says that you must empty the glass before you can refill it. After my frantic years in New York, I needed to do *nothing* before it could even occur to me what I might want to do next.

Day after day, I'd sit on my new porch, staring at the water or at the clouds in the sky. I'd wake up in the morning and realize to my delight that there was absolutely nothing I had to do that day. Of course, we were subsisting on savings and it couldn't go on forever, but so what? I was living for today, for *now*. Years before, I'd gone to hear a lecture by Alan Watts. That was what he had preached. Live for now, live in the moment, *now* is the only time there is. In Australia, I began to understand what he meant.

I decided I never wanted to pursue a career again, that at the age of forty-two, I'd become a drop-out. I sat down, examined our finances and found out that approximately 40 percent of what I earned got put aside, in one form or another, to ensure future security. We had life and fire insurance, retirement programs and annuities to send the kids to college.

I decided to cancel them all (and not have to earn that money). If the future wasn't real, why save for it? When Susie was old enough to go to Harvard, I'd probably be able to send her (and nothing would please me more). If I *couldn't* afford it, let her work her way through, or get a scholarship, or not go. I refused to sacrifice for her and then resent her for it. Rather than a guarantee of money for college, I'd bequeath her the memory of a contented father sitting on the porch with a can of Foster's Lager in his hand.

Life insurance, I decided, was a rip-off, where I was betting my hard-earned dough that I'd have the good fortune to get sick and die. And to hell with fire insurance. If the house burned down, I'd take it as a sign from God that it was time to move.

Meanwhile, life in Sydney wasn't bad and we could go on for quite a while without my working. The staples of life were cheap in Australia in 1970. Dinner for two at Maison Murph (our favorite restaurant) ran seven or eight bucks including wine. The best fruits and vegetables we'd ever eaten could be bought at the greengrocer for pennies, and the finest loin lamb chops in the world were 10¢ apiece. (Luxuries, on the other hand, were taxed to death. A refrigerator cost twice as much as it would have in the States. Fridges weren't considered necessities and in 1970 the average Aussie did not own one.)

We hadn't made many friends since our arrival in Australia. There was a young couple who lived up the street, and another from the country, named Jane and Max Patton. He was a veterinarian to the sheep farmers in the small town of Forbes, in the interior of New South Wales. We'd met them when they were on vacation in Sydney, and the four of us had hit it off. Subsequently, they'd invited us to fly to Forbes for a weekend of what they called Picnic Races. "It'll be a chance for you to meet some country people," said Jane Patton. "They're quite different from city folks; more sophisticated in certain ways." That surprised us. Back in the States, we explained, it was the other way around; we had city slickers and country bumpkins.

"Ah, but you see, traditionally the only Australians who could afford to travel were sheep farmers. That's where the money was. And travel does broaden. Most Aussies have an inferiority complex about their country. Those of us who spend time abroad learn to appreciate Australia, so we like ourselves better. But do come, Carolyn and Orson, and see for yourselves." We'd left the kids with Louise and flown in a commuter plane from the modern Sydney airport.

Forbes looked like a town out of the old west, Australia-style: dusty streets and buildings with false fronts. The Patton's charming place was off in the countryside, a rambling, sunny, Australian farm house, with dogs and cats wandering in and out of the kitchen. We were shown our room, unpacked the few things we'd brought with us, and then sat down to drinks on the Patton's veranda, where they filled us in on what we could expect for the weekend.

Picnic Races consisted of a day of amateur horse racing. People would drive for hundreds of miles to enter their horses in these races or to watch them. A pasture would be selected and an enormous ring created out of parked cars. Within this ring, the races would be held.

The cars were positioned facing out. The trunk of each car (Aussies, English-style, call it the *boot*) would be open and from it would be served sandwiches, cold chicken, beer and booze. The Picnic Races were an excuse for country folks to get together and party. Most people (there were perhaps 200 of them on our weekend) had arrived the day before the races and bunked in with friends. On Friday night, there were pre-race parties at houses all over the area. The Pattons took Carolyn and me to several of them and introduced us to their friends. Some of the parties went on all night. When they finally wound down, the people grabbed an hour's sleep or maybe two, and then it was time to head for the pasture.

The women, by and large, spent the day doling out food from the boots of their cars, gossiping with other women and keeping an eye on the children. The men wandered from car to car, helping themselves to ice cold cans of Foster's Lager or Bass Ale and cheering on their favorites in the races. In Australia in 1971, there was a substantial separation between the sexes. That may have changed by now, I don't know. Even in the homes of relatively sophisticated people, women would collect in one corner to make "lady talk," while men discussed football on the other side of the room. This was less true by far of the Forbes crowd, however, than it was in Sydney or Melbourne.

There were eight races on a typical Picnic Race day in Forbes. The only non-amateur element to the occasion consisted of a professional bookmaker, who would be flown down from Sydney to handle the betting. Aussies are great gamblers. The bookmaker at our Picnic Race was Alf Salmon. He had his name on a sign attached to the front of a little portable stand on which he perched, accepting bets and calling out the odds as they changed from moment to moment.

The odds on a given horse had a lot to do with the condition of the jockey as the day went by. By mid-afternoon, occasional riders were falling off their mounts, to hilarious acclaim from the sidelines. None of them seemed to get hurt, in the time-honored tradition of tumbling drunks. That night there were post-race parties at many of the same houses which had hosted the pre-race parties. The parties never ran out of beer, booze or food.

We made friends with a fellow house guest of the Pattons, a sheep farmer named Charles Edols. He was a craggily attractive man who lived by himself in a farm house a hundred miles away. His wife, from whom he was separated, lived in Sydney and he seemed to be carrying a bit of a torch for her. He drove a beat-up Mercedes. When the Pattons invited him for dinner, which they did frequently, he made the hundred-mile trip in a little over an hour. Most of the sheep people drove beat-up Mercedeses. It seemed to be an affectation, one that reminded me of Boston Brahmins and their old Brooks Brothers suits.

Or perhaps it was a variation of Aussie egalitarianism. Australians may unconsciously feel inferior to the rest of the world, but no Aussie feels inferior or superior to any other Aussie. The guy who waits on you in a shoe store is quite clearly your social equal. Presidents of corporations eat with their men in the company canteen, though at their own tables. I did a few Aussie TV shows and used to see the chairman of the board of Australia's largest television network come to work in a chauffeur-driven limousine. He sat up front with the driver. The back of the limo was always empty.

This feeling of equality, incidentally, did not extend to females. The chorus girls in *Promises, Promises* were paid 20 percent less than the chorus boys for doing exactly the same work. Australian Equity sanctioned this and neither sex seemed to take offense at the practice. This was in the early seventies. Maybe things have changed since, I don't know.

The post-race parties ended relatively early, by Aussie standards (three A.M.). Most people were exhausted from two days of non-stop drinking and eight hours of cheering or racing under the hot sun. On Sunday morning, after a few rounds of Bloody Marys (Carolyn, being pregnant, was not drinking), and a hearty Australian breakfast of bangers, eggs and lamb chops, our hosts asked if there were anything we'd like to see or do while we were still in the country. Carolyn said, "I've been in Australia for eight months now and I haven't seen a single kangaroo."

"We saw some at the zoo," I offered.

"I mean wild kangaroos," she said. "I want to see kangaroos in the wild." Our new friend Charles rose up with a yell.

"All off for the kangaroo tour." He lurched toward the door.

"Oh no," said Carolyn. "I'm not riding if any of you are driving. I want to live to have this Aussie baby of mine. *I'll* drive."

"Whoop," cried Charles. "A beautiful, pregnant, stateside bird for a chauffeur. Everyone into the car." Five of us crammed into Charles's Mercedes and took off, with Carolyn at the wheel. He had brought a bottle of Great Western Champagne, Australia's finest, and we passed it back and forth, drinking and laughing as it bubbled and spilled out on us.

"Turn here," Charles directed. "Now here." Suddenly the dirt road we were travelling on ceased to exist.

"What now?"

"Make a right around that big tree and keep going." Off the road we drove, crashing across a pasture, that gradually became a grove of trees, that gradually became woods.

"So this is why your cars look the way they do," said Carolyn.

"Around that rock—watch out for that log—to the left of that gum tree." Charles laughed uproariously. "You're great. Keep it up. You're doing fine. I've been this way before. We'll make it." We came to a large fallen tree and could go no farther. "This is good," said Charles. "Turn off the motor." We sat and waited. Above us, a cookaburra laughed insanely, scolding and clucking. Then Jane spoke, pointing out the left window of the Mercedes. "Look there. At the base of the big gum tree."

A creature out of *King Kong* was watching us. Slowly, authoritatively, with no hint of fear, an immense goanna sank his front claws into the trunk of the tree and pulled himself up, standing on his hind legs to have a better look at us. Then, satisfied that we were harmless, he proceeded to climb the great tree. A giant himself, he measured more than six feet from head to tip of tail. He moved up vertically and disappeared into the heavy overgrowth of leaves above us.

"Wow," I said quietly.

"Where are the kangaroos?" asked Carolyn.

"Be patient," said Charles. We waited and we waited. Half an hour went by.

"Forget it," said Max. "Let's go back. I need a drink."

"Shhh," said Charles. "Listen." I could hear nothing at first, then there was a distant thump, thump, thump, which gradually came closer. "It's a family," said Charles. "Be very quiet." Into the clearing on the other side of the fallen tree that had stopped us, no more than fifteen feet away, bounced a great buck kangaroo, six feet tall, his smaller, more delicate mate and three adorable joeys, each maybe two feet high on their great hind legs. Seeing the car, they stopped and stood completely still, eyeing us apprehensively, their beautiful soft brown eyes looking directly into ours. Perhaps a minute went by. Then, with a little nod of his head, the buck indicated that it was safe to continue and off they bounded into the woods.

We all sat very still. I had a lump in my throat and my eyes felt misty. I was sitting in the back of the Mercedes. I reached over to take Carolyn's hand in the driver's seat.

"Just a family out for a Sunday stroll," said Charles.

"Thank you for that, Charles," said Carolyn. "Now I feel I know Australia."

"C'mon, chauffeur. The bottle's empty and I'm dry. Back up and head around those bushes."

Our son was born at the King George V Hospital in Sydney in April, 1971. The bill for the entire stay, including private room for three days, use of all facilities and the finest medical care available anywhere was 56 bucks.

This without socialized medicine and with the doctors still driving big, fancy cars. How did they do it?

The hospital let me stay with Carolyn throughout the delivery, although they couldn't understand why I'd want to. The average Aussie husband is having one at the pub when his children are born. The entire hospital staff was completely relaxed, and there didn't seem to be the arbitrary rules that plague American hospitals. I sat next to Carolyn's bed in the labor room, eating a pizza and drinking a bottle of wine I'd brought with me. I helped her with her Lamaze breathing exercizes. They weren't widely known in Australia and the nurses regarded them with suspicion and some annoyance. They couldn't understand why Carolyn would want to be awake during the delivery or what I was doing there. Eccentric Americans.

After our son was born, Carolyn held him for a little while and then handed him to me and fell immediately into a deep sleep. I gazed down at the newest member of our family, then gave him over to a nurse's care and made my way home. I sat on the porch of our house and looked out at the harbor. I thought about the family of kangaroos we'd seen and I felt good.

We named the baby Ezekiel. With an older brother called Max, we figured he needed a good strong name. Ezekiel was an Old Testament prophet, the one who saw a giant wheel in the sky. Weeks went by and I waited for Carolyn to start feeling sexual again. My heart was beginning to ache. Here we were, having the time of our lives, touring the world, going through incredible changes and instead of its bringing us closer together, it seemed to be driving a wedge between us.

I was learning to let go (of fame, career and financial security). Back home in the States, the O'Neills' book *Open Marriage* was hot stuff. Maybe we needed to let go in our marriage. If we opened it up, perhaps the passion would come back into it. The more I thought about the idea, the better it seemed to me. (Remember, I was horny.) I broached the subject to Carolyn a few times, but was instantly rebuffed: "Forget it. No. Never. I'm not into that crazy stuff."

"Take a stand. Come off the fence. Are you interested or not?"

She couldn't even laugh at my jokes on the matter. She just kept imploring me to be patient, a quality for which I am not notorious.

One morning, when Zeke was out for a walk with Louise, Michele was at school and the other two kids had gone up the street to their friends' house to play, I decided that it was time to bell the cat. I took a deep breath, poured myself a cup of coffee, carried it into the living room and sat down on the floor with my back against the sofa. The French doors leading onto the porch were standing ajar. We were midway through our second Australian winter, but this time we were farther north in Sydney and the weather was mild.

After a while, as I knew she would, Carolyn noticed me there and came walking into the room.

"Why are you sitting on the floor?"

"I dunno. I guess I think better on the floor."

"What are you thinking about?"

"You and me. Us. And life."

"What's wrong with you and me?"

"Nothing's wrong. It's not a question of what's wrong. It's a question of what could be better." I patted the rug beside me and she walked over and sat down on it. "Darling, I love you."

"But what?" she asked warily.

"What do you mean?"

"You love me but what?"

"I don't love you but anything. I love you and there's stuff going through my mind that I need to talk with you about. And it's not easy." I shifted my position on the floor and took a sip of coffee. "I had a dream about sex last night." Carolyn's face turned pale.

"What about it?"

"I don't remember. It was just about sex. It was full of sexual images . . . of you, of me and of other people."

"What other people?"

"No other people in particular, just other people. It was about how there are lots of experiences to be had and that we're limiting ourselves."

"Who is it that you want to have sex with?"

"Darling. Listen to me. There's no one."

"Then why do you keep bringing up the subject?"

"My sweet woman. I know this is scary. It's scary for me too, even to think about, much less to talk about with my wife, whom I love more than anything in the world."

"Are you having sex with anyone now?"

Hopping up in annoyance, I stormed into the kitchen, carrying my coffee cup. Over the kitchen sink was a large window. Outside it, beneath the overhanging eave of the roof, a funnel-web spider had woven her elaborate, three-dimensional web. Now she waited for some unsuspecting, sex-crazed male to enter it for one last suicidal fling. (Or did I have my species wrong?)

Carolyn followed me into the kitchen.

"Damn it," I said as she came in. "Don't do this. No, I'm not having sex with anyone now. I'm with you practically 24 hours a day, for crying out loud. When the hell could I have sex with someone if I wanted to? And who the hell do I know worth having sex with in Australia? I'm talking about the fact that monogamy is an arbitrary social convention. Face it, honey, there must be other guys beside me who turn you on." Her face registered hurt.

"There aren't," she said. "I'm monogamous by nature. I always have been. I don't even look at other men sexually."

"That's the point. You don't look at them sexually so you don't see them sexually. You don't allow yourself to."

"Not everyone functions the way you do, Orson. Just because you want to go to bed with every woman you see, doesn't mean I operate the same way."

The charge was so absurd that I couldn't stay angry. I walked to her and took her in my arms. At first, she stayed stiff and unyielding, but finally she melted and tears began to run down her cheeks.

"I knew it would happen," she wept. "I knew you wouldn't have the patience to wait for me to get turned on again. And now you're saying you won't be satisfied with just me when I *do*."

I stroked her hair. "I'm greedy. I want us to have everything. Look. If you loved roast beef more than anything in the world, there'd still be times when you felt like eating popcorn, wouldn't there? Well, I want to be the prime rib of your life, but I'm saying it's OK sometimes for you to have popcorn. That won't take anything from me. It will just make you appreciate me more. If you never ate anything but roast beef, you'd get sick of it."

She disengaged herself from my arms, pulled a chair back from the kitchen table and sat down. "I don't understand," she said. "What is it you want us to do . . . go out and have affairs with other people?"

I perched on the chair next to hers. "I don't know, darling. The first thing we have to do is stick together in this and be open to change. If we don't do *something*, we're just going to drift apart." I reached over and took her hand. "I want us to feel close and excited again . . . closer than we've ever been in our lives."

"I want that too, Orson," she whispered. "I want us to have fun and adventure and the best sex life in the world . . . and I don't want to sleep with anyone but you."

She sat there, pale and anxious, and a wave of uncertainty swept over me. What was I pushing us into, and where would it lead? I loved her so much and needed to cherish and protect her. I slid my hand across the back of her chair and around her arm.

"Well, let's drop it for now," I said softly. "We're beating the subject to death. I'm taking you out to dinner tonight, alright?"

She smiled a little. "Yes Orson. Thank you." She got up. "I'm going next door to make sure the kids are OK." I watched her walk down the hall and go out the door. Then I sighed, stood up, stuck my empty cup in the sink and ran water into it. Carolyn would wash it later.

Miniskirts and over-the-knee boots were being worn in
Sydney that year, and when Carolyn was dressed and
ready to leave for our eight o'clock reservation, she looked
sexy and stunning. We kissed the kids goodnight, got in
our Australian Ford and drove to the nearby suburb of
Double Bay. Eliza's Garden was a new restaurant which
Carolyn had been wanting to try. It was romantic, the
food was acceptable and we felt good about having bothered to get dressed up to go out together.

When dinner was done, we sat sipping our leftover
wine. At a certain point I waved my arm to emphasize
some detail or other and knocked over the wine glass in
front of me. Then I watched in horror as its contents
drained directly into my lap.

"Oh God," said Carolyn, unable to hold back her
laughter. "Poor baby. Shall we go home?"

"No, damn it." My well-known stubbornness took over.
"I'm not going to let this ruin our evening."

"Well, the place is emptying out fast and we can't go
anywhere else with you in this condition. And the longer
you sit there, the bigger the wet spot is getting."

I managed to find no humor in the situation. "Look," I
said. "You go to the cocktail lounge in the other room
there and order us a couple of brandies." I reached into
the pocket of my sopping trousers and pulled out some of
my Australian play money to pay for the dinner bill. "I'll
drive home, whip on a dry pair of pants and be back in
twenty minutes."

"Twenty-five minutes minimum, but if that's what you
want, OK." I stood up and sloshed my way out of the restaurant. Carolyn sat at the table and finished her coffee.
Then she hailed the maître d' to ask for the check. When
he saw that her escort had apparently left for the evening,
a querulous look came over his face. For all its attempts
to keep up with the twentieth century, the remnant of the
British colonial system known as Australia is hopelessly
old-fashioned. A woman sitting alone in a restaurant at

night is a cause for general uneasiness and discomfort.

I managed to drive home in record time. Inside, I rushed to the bedroom, unzipping my pants as I went. I yelled an explanation to Louise, pulled on a pair of dry trousers, jumped in the car and was on my way back to Eliza's Garden. As I pulled into the nearly deserted parking lot, I glanced at my watch. Twenty-one minutes exactly. Smiling with satisfaction, I walked to the front of the restaurant and entered the door labeled "lounge." Inside I was greeted by a startling sight.

At the end of the bar sat my wife, alone. At the other end sat what looked like an entire rugby team. Each of the players was holding a glass of beer. At her end of the bar, Carolyn held nothing. The men were gazing intently at her, smirking to themselves and making whispered comments. Carolyn sat staring into the mirror behind the bar. When my reflection appeared in it next to hers, she turned, stood up, put her arms around me and gave me a passionate kiss. As she did so, an audible murmur of shock drifted up from the far end of the bar. I held her at arm's length and looked at her. I was a little shocked myself.

"What the hell's going on?" I asked. "Why haven't you ordered our drinks?"

"He won't take my order," she pouted. "He won't even look at me. He won't acknowledge my existence. I'm sure they all think I'm a hooker. God knows what they think you are. A john or my pimp or something. Decent people don't hug and kiss like that in public bars."

I laughed. "Is that why you gave me such a warm greeting?"

"No. It was because I was glad to see you. Get me a brandy, for God's sake."

When I glanced up, I saw that the spectators at the other end were all looking in our direction. Before the bartender had a chance to turn away, I signaled him and he came over, wearing a pleasant enough smile.

"The lady and I would each like a glass of cognac, please."

"Immediately, sir."

As he left, Carolyn leaned over to whisper in my ear. "To be honest, I guess I did hug and kiss you a little extra hard for their benefit. To hell with them. If they're going to gossip anyway, we might as well give them something to gossip about."

"You're too much," I laughed. Then I pulled back slightly to have a good look at her. "You do look a bit like a hooker in that outfit," I said. "A very expensive hooker."

The brandies arrived and we sat and drank them, glancing over from time to time to make sure the group was paying attention to us. After a while, we became aware of a conference of some sort going on. Then one of the men, who appeared slightly older than the rest, separated himself from the crowd and began inching his way closer to us. Ultimately, he found himself standing next to the barstool on our immediate right. The others remained behind, silently watching the new development.

"Another Foster's Lager, Mike," he called to the bartender. Then turning to me: "Can I offer you two a refill?"

"No thanks," I said. "It's very kind of you, but we've still got quite a bit left."

"American, are you?"

"Yes," I answered.

"No," answered Carolyn simultaneously. I quickly turned to look at her and spotted a devilish gleam in her eyes. "I'm Australian," she went on, imitating the accent quite well.

"Oh," replied the Aussie, looking at her as if for the first time, "and a very beautiful one at that." He allowed his eyes brazenly to take in her face and body, then turned back to continue his conversation with me.

"I've got a friend who lives in America," he said. "His home's in Little Rock. That's outside Chicago."

"The way Adelaide is outside Alice Springs," said Carolyn.

"What do you know about Adelaide?" The Aussie

looked at her directly.

"I'm *from* Adelaide," she answered. I stood dumb-founded, not knowing whether to laugh, cry or grab my wife and run.

"I know Adelaide very well." The Aussie was clearly warming to the conversation. "On every corner in Adelaide, there's either a church or a brothel."

"I'm from the brothel," said Carolyn with a straight face. I almost choked on my brandy and the Aussie almost choked on his beer. That was it; the fat was in the fire. Women in Australia never joke about such things. The lady was a hooker.

By this time, two of the boys from down the bar had managed to move closer, anxious to hear what was going on. Carolyn met each of their gazes. An excitement was building among them, and I was beginning to get nervous.

"C'mere." The Aussie pulled me a few feet away. "Look," he whispered. "The boys here have just finished training and are in town looking for a good time. We're with the Victoria League. They really admire the young lady and I'd like to work things out for them. Naturally, there'd be something in it for you." I glanced over my shoulder at Carolyn. She was now laughing and talking with the men, several more of whom had joined her.

"There's groups of us in town every week," the manager type went on, "and a lot of money to be made, with no effort on our part." Curiosity momentarily overcame my growing apprehension.

"How much money?" I asked.

"A thousand a week for us to split. Maybe more. And as I said . . . with no effort on our part."

"I'm afraid she's awfully tired tonight," I said, throwing some bills on the bar to pay for the drinks. "Perhaps some other night." I grabbed Carolyn's hand and pulled her off the barstool.

"Wait a minute," cried the Aussie, his face darkening. "Where are you going? Are you on the phone? What's your number?"

"Not on the phone yet," I called as we headed for the door. "Just arrived in town. See you back in here sometime." We were out on the sidewalk by then, howling with laughter.

"You really are bad," I said, when we were finally safe inside the car.

"That's right. That's what I am. I'm bad."

"I'm taking you home, dressed like that. I don't dare walk around with you. I'll open us a bottle of Great Western. Then I'll have at you myself. And I'm not paying."

"We'll see," said Carolyn. "We'll see how good the champagne is.

We slept late the morning after the rugby affair, then woke up feeling close and liberated. Things seemed to have fallen into perspective: we'd experienced that sex didn't always have to be heavy and "meaningful," that sometimes it could be just plain fun (or just fancy fun).

But inevitably, the pendulum began to swing back towards negative. As the day wore on, Carolyn started to feel depressed and put upon.

"You probably would have liked it if I'd gone off with that crowd of slobs from Melbourne," she hissed.

"Damn it, Carolyn . . ." I wholeheartedly plunged into my half of the Apache dance. "You certainly seemed to enjoy it at the time. You batted your eyes at them and accepted all the strokes they were throwing your way."

"Well I sure didn't intend to do anything about it. Frankly, I just thought my little act would turn you on. You'd worn me down, for God's sake, so I figured, 'Alright, I may as well give him his fantasy.'"

I sulked as Carolyn seethed and the good, close, excited feelings faded away. Finally, I got bored with the game and decided to stop my part of it. I waited till dinner was over, the kids had been tucked in and Louise had gone to her room to watch a rerun of *Peyton Place* on TV. Then I poured two glasses of wine and carried them to the back porch.

A little kumquat tree stood in an earthenware pot next to the railing and I noticed that the last of its fruit was gone. The possum who lived in the attic had polished the kumquats off, a few each night, until now the tree was bare. It was a warm evening and a large cruise ship sat at anchor in the harbor directly across from our house. A string of lights ran from its bow up to and across its twin smokestacks and then down to the stern. The effect was lovely and romantic.

I placed the wine glasses down on the railing next to the potted tree and called to Carolyn to join me.

"What do you want?" She came glowering out of the house.

"I've had enough of our staying away from each other, that's all."

"So?"

"So I think we should talk."

"What's there to say? You want us to run around hopping in and out of bed with people, and I'm just not interested. That's that, and I don't know what to do about it."

"Jesus." I shook my head in disbelief. "When you decide to retrench, you certainly do go all the way back, don't you. Look, I don't want to waste a lot more time on this issue, but just let me reiterate that I am not in favor of our hopping in and out of bed with people. What I am in favor of is allowing ourselves a choice in the matter. Freedom to say yes means freedom to say no. It implies selectivity."

"But I don't want to go to bed with anyone but you. That's what you can't seem to understand or accept. I just managed to whip myself up for your benefit."

"And did you whip up the loving closeness that followed it? That's what you have to ask yourself, Carolyn. We felt more love and excitement last night than we have all year. Do you agree?" She said nothing for a while, then nodded her head reluctantly. She sipped at the wine I'd brought out for her, then bent over to scoop up a half-eaten kumquat from the deck and pitch it over the railing into the bushes. She stood there, small and frightened, wrestling with her pride. Finally, she looked into my eyes.

"I feel scared," she said.

"I know," I answered softly. "I feel scared too, sometimes; scared of what I may find out about myself . . . or rather, of what I imagine I may find out. But to hell with it . . . I'm willing to take the chance. If there's a mass murderer somewhere inside me, or a killer rapist or a child molester . . . damn it, I want to know. I won't go on being out of touch with beautiful things inside me for fear I may find terrible things in there, too."

"But it makes us so vulnerable . . . and I can't help it, I don't want to get hurt."

I took her in my arms. She let me do so, but her pride wouldn't allow her to give in yet.

"Look," I said. "I'll never try to talk you into anything you don't want to do. I just need us to get in touch with what we really *do* want and not go on kidding ourselves anymore. I want us to be open to *everything*. Maybe we'll . . ." I looked around in desperation. "Maybe we'll wind up with the possom from the attic."

The laughter poured out of her involuntarily. "Please," she begged. "Not the possom. You saw what he did to the kumquats." She looked at me for a moment, then hung her head. "Alright," she said in a barely audible whisper. "Alright. Just don't make me nervous by talking about it all the time." I laughed long and hard, holding her closely.

"Come on," I said at last. "Let's go to bed and make love. No rugby team, no possom from the attic . . . just you and me. Right now I don't want to share you with anyone."

Carolyn was tired. Giving birth to Zeke had taken more out of her than she knew. Dealing with my madness had added to her fatigue. To make matters worse, after fifteen sparse months, our social life suddenly began to boom. Seemingly from out of nowhere, we were inundated with invitations to cocktail parties and dinners.

It began with a call from a doctor and his English wife, whom we had met some months before, but never heard from since.

"We were just thinking about you two and wondered if you'd come to a party at our place this Saturday. There'll be some people here you'd enjoy meeting."

The people turned out to be the owners of a well-known chain of fashion boutiques. He was Hungarian, she Australian, and both of them were fascinating. We spent the evening talking with them, then found ourselves invited to their house the following night. There, we met another captivating couple, he English, she Australian. And they in turn asked us over to their place "to meet a few good friends."

From social hermits, we evolved into "the couple in demand," the center of an ever-increasing circle of alluring admirers.

"These new friends of ours are mesmerizing," I said to Carolyn one day.

"A strange choice of words."

"Well, aren't they? I mean, they're so full of energy. And they seem to be interested in so many curious, offbeat things."

"Hmm."

"What do you mean hmm?"

"I guess I mean I don't trust them. They seem too good to be true. Where did they come from all of a sudden? And why are they sweeping us off our feet? I almost get the feeling we're being wooed."

"God," I grumbled. "We hardly have any friends at all for a year. Now we make some really interesting ones and you're complaining."

"Well, we'll see," she said. "We'll see."

At a party one night, she broke down and invited two of the women to have lunch at our house.

"Oh good," said one. "I can't wait to see what you've done with that dreadful old place."

There was an awkward pause, then Carolyn said, "Oh?

Have you been in our house before?"

The woman averted her eyes. "No," she answered. "I just know it was boarded up for a long time."

It didn't ring true.

That night at bedtime, Carolyn was close to tears. "I don't trust any of them. It's the way they look at me. Their eyes. They seem to go right inside my mind. I feel as if they could make me do anything they wanted . . . tell them anything they wanted to hear."

"Look, you're tired. This is all subjective stuff. I don't feel any of it. You're really acting nutsy. Get some sleep."

Thus was my husbandly concern expressed.

We fell asleep, but then suddenly she was awake again, or half awake, sitting up in the dark in our bed and saying the words, "Which numbers?"

"What?" I awoke from an equally deep sleep.

"Which numbers?"

"What the hell are you talking about?"

"Which numbers?" she insisted.

I wracked my brain for an answer. For some reason my heart was pounding. Then, from deep down in my unconscious, I answered, "666."

She looked terrified. "What is that?"

"Jesus, Carolyn, I don't know. You asked me which numbers and I said the first thing that popped into my mind. It's the address of the Tishman Building, back home in New York: 666 Fifth Avenue."

"What else is it?"

I hesitated. The room was deathly still as she sat waiting for me to speak. Reluctantly then, I gave the other answer: "It's an evil number. The mark of the beast. From the Book of Revelations."

She hissed with a sudden intake of breath. "How do you know something like that?"

"I don't know. I just know it. I know a lot of useless shit like that. My father told me when I was a kid."

She reached out and clutched my forearm tightly. "Do you want to know what else it is? It's the address of Maison Murph, 666 New South Head Road. That's where all these new friends of ours hang out. And it's where the doctor who owned this house used to go. Murph told me." The hair rose on the back of my neck. "You may think I'm cracking up but I feel this inside. They're doing something to control us. I don't know how and I don't know why, but I know it's true. They're lying to us and manipulating us. They've been in this house before, all of them. The first time I ever set foot in here I knew something evil had gone on in the place." She paused, then asked: "Which two countries do you associate with witchcraft?"

By now I wasn't quite so quick to pooh pooh her fears. "I don't know. England and, I guess, Hungary."

"Alright," said Carolyn. "At least one member of every couple we've met lately is either English or Hungarian. The doctor who owned this house was Hungarian and the locks he put on all the doors were to keep people out . . . or in. He died here and no one seems to know exactly how, but there's something we're not being told."

Her eyes involuntarily glanced at the wall behind me. I looked around and saw something I hadn't noticed before: two wooden matches scotch-taped together in the form of a cross.

"What the hell is that?"

"It's for protection," she said. "Leave it. There's one over Zeke's crib, too." She sat there, looking drained and miserable in the faint reflection of the baby's night light, filtering in from the door to the nursery next to our bedroom.

"I have to go to the john," she said.

"So go."

"I want you to walk there with me."

"What? It's fifteen feet away."

"I know it sounds crazy, but I want you to walk me there and wait by the door till I come out. I'm terrified."

Exasperated, not knowing whether to feel foolish or protective or both, I got up, took her trembling hand and escorted her across the hall to the bathroom. She went in, then locked the door behind her. A sliver of light came from under it as she clicked on the wall fixture. I waited outside.

Suddenly, something caught my attention. I felt its presence before I saw it . . . knew that something was standing at the end of the hall, watching me. I peered into the darkness, then turned away, shook my head and looked back again. It was there . . . something blacker than the black, and now it began to move, slowly gliding toward me. The hall grew cold, perceptibly colder. An involuntary shudder ran through me and the blood drained out of my face. I felt fear . . . more fear than I could ever remember experiencing. Terror immobilized my body. Closer the thing came, and now I could make out a shrouded, faceless form . . . a presence that seemed to me the embodiment of pure evil.

Then, as quickly as my fear had come, it disappeared and a feeling of righteous anger replaced it. I took a step toward whatever it was.

"Get the hell out of here," I said quietly, almost in a whisper. "This is my house and I will not be driven from it." The thing paused, remained suspended in front of me for an instant, then slowly began to pull back.

Behind me, I heard the bolt slide on the bathroom door. Then the door opened and Carolyn came out. As she did, the light from behind her fell on my face. She gasped.

"What's happened?" she whispered. I shook my head, unwilling to answer her. "You've seen something," she insisted, "haven't you . . . haven't you?"

"Alright," I said. "I have."

"What was it?"

I gave no response.

"Was it a black, spectral thing wrapped in a shroud?"

I gaped at her in astonishment. When I could finally speak, I said, "Yes. It's gone now."

"But it will be back. I've seen it every night for the past week. It comes at four A.M. and hovers over the baby's crib. He wakes up and that wakes me and I see it through the nursery door. Oh Orson, I'm so frightened."

"Why in the name of God haven't you told me?"

"Because you already think I'm paranoid about these people. I was afraid to." She fell sobbing into my arms. "I've never asked you for a lot," she said, "but I'm asking for something now. I don't want to spend one more night in this house or in this country." I held her and felt a wave of love sweep over me. She seemed so small and helpless.

"Alright darling, alright my dearest. I guess it's time for us to move on anyway."

We turned all the lights on and started packing. In the morning, I called Pan Am and booked us on the afternoon flight. The children woke up. "We're going home, kids," we told them. We gave the poor, startled Louise a month's pay and offered to let her stay on in the house until she found another job. There were piles of clothing in every room.

"Take what things you want and give the rest to the Salvation Army," we told her. All we kept was blue jeans. "Call Fred Weston and tell him to put the house on the market. Ask him to have Grace Brothers come for the furniture. We'll write when we know where it's to be sent."

We didn't tell her about You Know Who. He'd probably never bother her, we figured. If he did, she could move out, the way we did.

We were going home to America!

VIII

On a pitch black night in March 1986, an astro-physicist named Edwin Turner is looking through the giant 158-inch reflecting telescope at the Kitt Peak Observatory in Arizona, when he discovers something which makes his eyes pop. He doesn't know what it is; a cluster of galaxies perhaps. But it is at a greater distance than anything yet found in the cosmos: 5 *billion* light years away. And it is unimaginably huge: a thousand times bigger than our Milky Way (which consists of hundreds of billions of stars, of which our sun is a relatively small one).

This is only the beginning. The best telescope we have is a Tinkertoy. In the future, we'll find stuff that makes this new thing look like a gum wrapper. Einstein used to get a faraway look in his eyes and say, "There's something else out there." He didn't want to talk about God and lose his credentials. He hesitated to consider (out loud) the possibility that we are figments of an Imagination, that everything we experience may be taking place in Someone's dream.

The more adventurous of the New Physicists suggest

that everything that has ever happened, ever will happen or ever *may* happen is in fact, happening right now. There is scientific theory that hints at this possibility. Reality is not what we believe it to be. (Or said another way: Reality *is* what we believe it to be.)

I stand in my bachelor cottage listening to the ducks quack outside in the canals, and quieting the roof chatter in my mind. I begin to grin. Now I'm chuckling out loud. The whole thing is so sweet and funny. Time is riding off in all directions, that new Galaxy Cluster would look swell on my mantelpiece . . . and Carolyn and I are on our way home to America.

Venice, California, 1987

IX

We laughed on and off all the way across the Pacific. It was late August, midwinter, when we left Australia and we'd be back in New York for the end of summer.

The plane set down in Honolulu and we had to clear U.S. Customs and Immigration. I hadn't known what to write on the forms I'd filled out. Under occupation I put "house husband." I had become a drop-out. I wondered whether I'd still be able to work on TV, on the talk and game shows. I didn't know if anyone in the States would remember me. The immigration officer looked up from his forms in Honolulu. "Oh, Mr. Bean," he said. "Good to see you. My wife watches you every day on *To Tell the Truth.*

Carolyn guffawed. "You were afraid they wouldn't remember you," she said. "They didn't even know you were gone."

We flew on to L.A., stopping there for a couple of days to take the kids to Disneyland. *My* amusement parks, after fifteen months in Australia, were the shopping malls.

To go into a K Mart and see miles and miles of consumer goods . . . it was the best and worst of America. No more eggs wrapped in newspaper.

On to New York then, where we bunked in with friends. We still had our little beach house in Westhampton and decided to stay there till we figured out our next move. The other property we owned was an apartment at the Palm Bay Club in Miami. Fancy. We'd bought it from plans as an investment a few years previous, and work on the building had begun while we were Down Under. We figured it should be nearly complete by now, and wrote Fred Weston to ship our furniture there.

We needed wheels. I walked out into the street in New York and the first thing I saw was a parked '61 VW van with a sign in its window that read FOR SALE, $600. The perfect vehicle for an aging hippy. I ran back inside for Carolyn. A guy with a beard and sandals came from the house where the van was parked and told us that he owned the car.

"Will you take $500?"

"Sure."

"Does it run?"

"Yeah. Hop in and spin it around the block." We consummated a deal on the spot.

The next day, we drove the van to Westhampton and moved into our house. Carolyn had insisted we hold on to it, a year and a half before, when we were ready to leave for Australia and I'd been in a mood to dump everything. The place was beachy and cozy, with a brick fireplace: sliding glass doors led onto a large deck, which extended smack down to the edge of Peconic Bay.

The post-Labor Day exodus had taken place, and we were basking in Indian Summer. The sunsets were phenomenal. As September passed and turned into October, great flying wedges of southbound ducks and geese would put down to rest on the bay in front of our house. A family of swans, which lived year 'round in the Hampton waterways, swam to our deck every day, begging for food. They accepted bread, but preferred dry cat food, which we began to stock for them.

Our heads were still spinning from all that had come down in Australia. For a long time, Carolyn didn't even want to talk about the ghost. The first thing she did when we moved into the house at Westhampton was to dig out our old Ouija Board and burn it in the fireplace. "Stuff like that doesn't strike me as cute any more," she said.

I had a theory about our visitor, which I expounded on to Carolyn: Einstein had proven that matter is nothing but energy, spinning around in some funny way that gives it the appearance and feel of solidity. In Sydney, we (with the aid of our friends, the possible coven) had whipped up a houseful of negative energy; and this energy had somehow congealed into a form, the shape of which had been created by our shared unconscious (with the help of Charles Dickens, Bram Stoker and Stephen King).

Carolyn's view of the episode was less cerebral: we had been living in a haunted house. The ghost, she believed, was the Hungarian doctor, who may have been an abortionist. This, she said, could account for all the locks on the doors.

Whoever was right, the spook had done no harm, but had in fact performed a service by making us realize that our Aussie adventure was over, and it was time to go home.

We settled in to our little cottage at the beach and made love and made love. We felt close and happy. Opening up our relationship would now have seemed superfluous. Simply having accepted the possibility turned out to have been enough. We were as amorous as honeymooners. We shared fantasies, experimented with different kinds of love making, and couldn't seem to get enough of each other. Sometimes, when our eyes met, waves of excitement would pass between us. The touch of fingers on skin produced electric shocks of pleasure. We seemed to have connected on a whole new level. The kids picked up on all the energy and happiness, and the family became closer knit than ever.

We drove up to Vermont to see old Grandpa. Till he was ninety-four, he had lived alone in his house in Hartland. Then, he'd reluctantly agreed to move into the old folks' home in nearby Windsor. Once there, he enjoyed himself thoroughly because there were lots of women (of various ages) to keep him company. He was glad to see us and delighted with his beautiful great-grandchildren. We drove him the few miles to Hartland to spend an afternoon in his old house. The place had originally been a summer home when my grandparents had lived up north in Burlington. Later, they had insulated it and gone to live there full time.

Grandpa puttered around, looking at this and that, inspecting his furniture, happy to be back, checking papers in his desk, each one stirring a memory. To be there with him brought childhood summers flooding back to me. I left him at his desk and walked out onto the back porch where the family used to eat summer dinners. The family had been my mother and me and her parents. My father seldom came to Vermont, though I often urged him to. I had dreams of familial harmony but in fact there was little love lost between him and his in-laws, who apparently felt that their daughter had married beneath her station (whatever that was).

Standing on the porch, I looked down the hill at Grandpa's old vegetable garden, a small portion of which was still being cultivated by a neighbor. The big cornfield and most of the rest of it had been allowed to go to seed. When I was little and the garden was in full flower, Grandpa would put a huge pot of water on the wood stove in the kitchen. After the water had come to a boil, he would send me out to collect two dozen ears of the succulent, sweet, pale yellow corn he grew. Pulling out his old railroad watch, he would raise his right hand. I'd stand at the edge of the porch by the steps leading down the hill to the garden, poised, ready to race.

"If the corn isn't husked and in the pot within five minutes of being picked," he'd say, "it's not worth eating." He'd glace at his watch, then lower his hand. "Go."

And off I'd fly.

There were daily and weekly chores I had to perform each summer in Hartland . . . lugging wood from the wood-shed to the kitchen stove or the pot belly in the parlor, mowing and raking the grass, clearing the table after meals and washing the dishes. In the dog days of August, I'd be paid five cents a hundred to kill flies with a red rubber fly swatter. My grandparents, fun loving in some ways, were Calvinist in their work ethic. The fact that my father had a job with the W.P.A. was one of the reasons they held him in low esteem.

My grandmother objected to my collection of Captain Marvel comics and gave me picture books of the life of Jesus and cautionary tales from Aesop. *The Grasshopper and the Ant* was one of my unfavorites. Naturally, I identified with the grasshopper who wanted to fiddle around all summer while the red ant slaved. The book had a picture of the grasshopper in winter, his threadbare green coat clutched around his skinny shoulders, freezing, pleading at the ant's door to be taken in. "No," calls the ant from inside, cozy at his roaring fire. "You played while I worked. Now you must suffer the consequences." Death, I wondered? Can life really be that cruel? But every summer in Hartland there were just as many grasshoppers hopping around as there had been the year before. Something was crazy. I was learning not to trust the grownups. (Later, they took me to see Disney's *Three Little Pigs*. When the wolf terrorizes the pigs by blowing down the house of straw and the house of sticks, the diligent, humorless pig with the house of bricks takes his indigent brothers in. Moral? Work hard, plan ahead and you get to look after the poor.)

The screened-in porch where we ate the corn I picked had been added on to the place one summer and had become the center of family life. At the end of the day, Grandpa loved to sit on it with his drink and watch the sun go down over his garden and the little brook and swimming hole beyond it. During my earliest years in Hartland there was no indoor plumbing. An outhouse occupied the space where the porch now stood, attached to the main wall, with a little stoop in front of it leading to the kitchen. A fine, family-style three-holer it was, with two adult-sized facilities and a smaller kiddie seat. It was not unusual in those days for several members of a farm family, after meal time, to retire to the privy together. Country people seem to be, for the most part, completely uninhibited about their bodily functions, neither requiring nor respecting privacy. Perhaps this is because they've grown up with farm animals.

There was a wooden box of dirt in our outhouse with a pan stuck in it. When one's "necessaries" were completed, one scooped out a panful or two of the dirt and tossed it down the opening, to the angry buzzing of the flies who lived in the dreadful cavern beneath it. This was a good eight feet deep, due to the facility's being constructed on the side of a fairly steep incline. Every two weeks or so, it became one of my jobs to get my red wagon out, place the wooden box on it, trudge the quarter of a mile or so up the road to the county gravel pit and replenish the supply of dirt. I despised this job more than any of the other chores I had, including the slaughter of the flies, at a nickle a hundred, which the three-holer seemed to attract.

At the end of each summer, old man Osgood would arrive from North Hartland in a wagon pulled by a sleepy nag. He would pry open the door at the base of the outhouse and shovel out the whole terrible mess. He charged nothing for this service because he claimed that human waste was a finer fertilizer than any, and he was happy to have it. He always brought along a load of pumpkins for my grandmother, boasting that they were bigger and tastier than those of any other farmer, due to his unique form of fertilization. I didn't care for the pies my grandmother produced from his gift. This recycling of our energies disturbed my delicate Boston sensibilities.

Sometimes my grandparents went to the outhouse together. It was hard for me, a city boy, to imagine the attraction of john-sharing, but looking back, it seems that

whatever it was, it was symptomatic of an intimacy
which allowed a marriage to continue and grow for 60
years.

Inhibited or uninhibited, country people love their
toilet humor. Certainly my grandparents did. The three-
holer was a source of constant ribald merriment to them.
They hung a chain in there one year, with a handle on
the end of it, and told visitors they'd installed a newfan-
gled water flush. The chain was in fact attached to an old
church bell on the roof, which gramp had picked up at an
auction in Woodstock. The neighbors across the street and
next door were in on the gag, and would come out to
cheer whenever an unsuspecting dinner guest gave a yank
on the chain.

There was no plumbing at all in the house, not even a
faucet in the kitchen. Water was drawn from a well in the
yard near the front of the barn. I remember the excitement when an indoor pump was finally installed, with
pipes running to it from a cistern. A small primer pitcher
stood next to it and when I occasionally forgot to fill it
after pumping a glass of water for myself, I had to go and
draw a bucket from the well, a prospect which filled me
with dread. Wells were things little kids got pushed down
in the Grimms' Fairy Tales I still read. Eventually, some
years later, my grandparents broke down and had hot and
cold running water and a bathroom installed.

Lee Graham, the local contractor, was engaged for the
job of moving the outhouse intact, 25 feet away down the
wall toward the carriage house, and then constructing the
enclosed porch which would lead to it. When the work
was completed, a big party was thrown to inaugurate the
new addition. The three-holer was freshly painted in red,
white and blue stripes. Fifty to sixty people came to the
party. My grandparents' parties were very social and
always hugely successful. The booze flowed freely and
there was plenty of good food. I was given a medal to
wear indicating the importance of my function as replen-
isher of the gravel. I ran around excitedly, playing with
the other kids who had come to the party with their

parents. My father had written, in response to the invitation, that he'd try to make it up from Cambridge, but he hadn't been able to.

By the end of summer, in the August heat, it was discovered that the social usefulness of the porch was severely limited by its proximity to the three-holer, and plans were made that when my grandparents closed up the house and returned to Burlington, Lee Graham would move it still farther away, completely out of sight this time inside the old carriage house. I never felt comfortable around Lee Graham, a good-looking rugged individual, because I had deduced from snatches of overheard conversation that he had been an old boyfriend of my mother's. There seemed to be an element of flirtation between them still and insecure as I was about my parents' marriage, anything that I could imagine as threatening to it worried me.

When my mother and I returned to Hartland the following summer, the further renovation had been completed. The back-porch now had a view where the old outhouse had stood . . . and that facility was located in the carriage shed. This could be reached by going through a rear room called the doctor's office, which apparently had functioned as such when a previous owner had lived in the house during the last century.

The recurrent moving of the old outhouse had resulted in a minor catastrophe. The small child-sized seat had cracked and then fallen apart, and we now had only a two-holer. My grandparents decided to hold a funeral for the broken toilet.

Lee Graham generously constructed a small coffin, with handles on the sides and a glass top, through which the broken child-sized third hole could be seen. Guests, over a hundred of them, were instructed to wear mourning clothes. One fool, a fat guy named Woody, came dressed as a clown. Several members of the high school band were engaged, traffic was stopped and a large procession paraded through town, lead by the band and the pall bearers carrying the small casket. The burial took place behind the barn, after which the mourners retired to the house for the festive wake.

Later in the summer a mock trial was held. Woody, the guy in the clown suit, was falsely charged with breaking the small appliance by sitting down on it too hard, but ultimately a conviction was gotten of my mother's old boyfriend. This secretly pleased me. Though on one level I enjoyed all these events as the theme parties they were, on another level I took them seriously and felt the loss of the little toilet.

The festivities at my grandparents' home were an on-going celebration of life. Grandmother directed a fully costumed production of *Winnie the Pooh* in the barn. I made my theatrical debut in this, appearing in the role of Roo. They played cut-throat bridge far into the night with friends and neighbors. They gave dinner parties and brunches. They served pitchers of lemonade and iced tea, and helped me make Kool Aid. Once a week they baked fresh bread in the oven and fried donuts in a cauldron on the stove. The house was alive and filled with excitement. But in the autumn, of course, I always had to go home.

We drove Grandpa back to the residence, tired and happy. Carolyn took the kids to McDonald's while I saw the old man to his room. He was ninety-five now and in good shape, but it was obvious he couldn't go on forever. I asked him what his feelings were about dying. He thought for a moment, then said to me: "When you were a little fella and it was your bedtime, you'd put up a helluva fight. Even though you were tired and rubbing your eyes, you didn't want to go to sleep. You were afraid you'd miss something. When you got older and it was the end of a long day and you'd had fun, I used to tuck you in and you'd say how nice the cool pillow felt on your face. Well, I've had fun and don't feel I've missed anything, and I look forward to going to sleep."

I settled in to my role as stay-at-home husband. Feminists say housework is demeaning. It liberated me.

Vacuuming became my *thing*. I became Lord of the Electrolux. When I had finished a vast expanse of carpet and all the little threads were going in the same direction, I felt like an Iowa wheat former surveying his fields. Then, the job completed, I'd switch off the vacuum . . . and now it's Miller time.

We decided to stay at the beach through Christmas and then head down to Miami. Our little house was not insulated or heated, other than by the fireplace, so we hired a local guy to put in a furnace and I set about the business of winterizing the place, tacking rolls of fiberglass between the studs and then cutting, fitting and nailing up new interior walls. Outside, along the edge of the water, prehistoric horseshoe crabs mated, the small males attempting to pry one another off the larger, more imposing females.

Evenings at the beach came earlier and earlier as we approached the midwinter solstice: December 22nd, the shortest day of the year. The kids and I went out collecting driftwood late one afternoon, then stopped to watch the sun go down over Peconic Bay, a sight which invariably thrilled us. The air was balmy for December. The ocean with its salt breezes is a natural insulator; the area around the shore is always cooler in summer and warmer in winter.

"Thousands of years ago," I said as we trudged along the beach, "a family like ours may have stood right here where we are now, watching the sunset and saying ooh and aah, or whatever the caveman equivalent of that was. And maybe they wondered why the big ball of fire was getting smaller and smaller in the December sky. Of course they didn't call it December. They didn't call it anything. They didn't have calendars or need them. They knew things deep inside, by instinct, that we've forgotten how to know. But one thing they didn't know back then was whether or not the sun would keep on getting smaller and finally go away for good one day. They understood that if that happened the world would come to an end: no more mammoth hunts, no more rock-dropping parties, no more dragging cave women off by the hair. Nothing.

"On the day we now call December 22nd, the sun gets really small and pale and far away, and our poor cave family on the beach must have thought, 'Well boys, this is it.' But by the next day, the sharpest-eyed guy in the tribe, maybe the medicine man or the head rock-dropper, took a look and told himself that the sun hadn't gotten any farther away. By the 24th, he was pretty sure he was right and he was all excited, but still he didn't say a word because if you announced something like that and it turned out not to be true, the tribe played funny tricks on you like feeding you to sabre-toothed tigers.

"But on the 25th of December the guy was convinced that the sun was coming back so he told everyone in the clan . . . and they looked up and saw that it was true. Well, talk about a party . . . extra Pterodactyl for everyone, and dancing and people giving rocks to each other. So a celebration on December 25th is programmed into our unconscious tribal memory. It's the day when we all know, deep down inside, that everything is going to be alright.

"And that's why we have Christmas at this time of year. We don't know when that sweet little Babe was born in the manger, but it was probably in the spring, because that's when his mom and dad . . . well, one of his dads . . . had gone to Jerusalem to pay their taxes. For the first few centuries of Christianity, Jesus' birthday was never celebrated on December 25th. That had become a pagan holiday and those were a no-no with the big shots of the church. But deep inside, all the people including the big shots felt good on that day, and needed to show love and to share and exchange presents and have folks over for dinner. So finally the church gave in and decided to celebrate Christ's birthday on the 25th. And that's why we all love each other especially around this time of year . . . and it's also why Mr. Hasbro and Mr. Mattell are so rich."

On the day after Christmas we clambered into the van and set out for Miami. We moved into our apartment, celebrated the New Year there, then enrolled the older kids in the local school and settled in for the winter. We spent the following summer back in Westhampton, then migrated south again for a second winter. We were an anamoly among the idle rich at Miami's fashionable Palm Bay Club: the idle voluntary poor. I had grown a beard and wore work shirts. The '61 VW van with the Mickey Mouse wallpaper stood out among the Cadillacs and Mercedeses. Ever four or five weeks, I flew to L.A. to appear on *The Tonight Show*. While I was there, I'd knock off a week's worth of *The Match Game* or some other panel show, then fly home and we'd live for the next month on what I'd earned. I had, as I used to say: "Enough money to last the rest of my life, provided I die a week from Thursday."

We decided to spend the winter of '73–'74 up north at the beach house. On Dune Road in the winter, our nearest neighbor would be a mile away. As an experiment, I wanted to see how cheaply we could live, without experiencing actual discomfort. We were existing in the financial *now*, with very little put away for the future. If a building fell on me, the family would have to get by with a lot less money. Would that be OK? I wanted to find out.

We started buying house-brand rice krispies at the A & P in Westhampton because they were six cents cheaper than Kellogg's. We gave up TV because the cable cost fifteen dollars a month. The kids suffered as they went cold turkey from The Flintstones, and ditto their dad with no Walter Cronkite. But in a week or so, a great feeling of peace descended on the house. I even stopped buying the daily paper, as I began to realize how irrelevant the news of the world was to my actual life.

The kids and I would go to the beach every morning to collect driftwood. At night, we'd burn it in the fireplace and read aloud in front of the fire. The fireplace provided warmth and a social gathering place. Once a week, I'd take the family out for pizza and a movie, and every so often, Carolyn and I would visit Papa Joe's Bar, drink wine and play the bowling machine.

Max, at the age of seven, developed the annoying habit of waking up in the middle of the night and crawling into bed with us. We let him stay a few times, hoping he'd get it out of his system. When he continued, we firmly carried him back to bed and let him squawk.

One night, we came home drunk and horny from an evening at Papa Joe's. We inadvertently left the door to our bedroom standing open and all the lights on. Then we tore each other's clothes off and for some reason started making love on the bedroom floor. Five minutes later, the chianti wore off sufficiently for me to become aware of a third presence in the room.

I looked around and there he stood, wearing his Dr. Denton's and a grin as broad as the Snake River Canyon. It was obvious he'd been there from the beginning. Not being able to think of anything else to do, I climbed off his mother and we got into bed and pulled the blankets over ourselves. Then I patted the edge of the bed and motioned for him to come and sit down on it.

"Your mom and I love each other very much," I said, "and when people love each other, it feels good for them to make love."

Carolyn said: "When you're older, you'll probably have a girlfriend and make love with her yourself."

His grin got even broader. "Can I sleep with you?" he asked.

"No, boy," I answered, "The show's over. You've seen it all." He went back to his bed and that was the end of his nocturnal wanderings. He never came to us in the night again. He'd seen what he needed to see.

As Christmas time approached, we told the kids that we weren't going to load everyone up with useless items from Hasbro and Ideal that year. Rather, we said, we were all going to make things for one another, in the manner of an old-fashioned Christmas. There was the obligatory grumbling but soon enough it was replaced by the delight of whispered conferences and planning. I helped the kids make stuff for their mother, she helped them with presents for me, and the older ones helped the younger ones make things for their brothers and sisters.

On Christmas morning there was no frantic littering of the living room floor with useless and unwanted toys, but rather a simple and heartfelt exchange of gifts and genuine affection. We all remember it as our favorite Christmas ever.

We got word that winter from my cousin Gerald in Vermont that old Grandpa had finally died. He'd made it to ninety-seven and then given up the ghost. The last time I'd spoken to him, he'd said that he'd had about enough: "All my friends are dead and the women don't take me seriously any more." He was the dearest man I've ever known.

Spring came to the beach and by then we'd learned that what most people think of as necessities are really luxuries, that love and good times together are what count. When I read about families where "both mother and father have to work, just to make ends meet," I wonder how many children come home to an empty house with a color TV in it.

But having proved our point to ourselves, we all agreed that enough was enough of the Spartan life. We could do it if we had to, and even *like* it (and if anything happened to Dad, the rest of the family would be fine). But it really suited us to live a little higher on the hog. I was sick of commuting to California and wanted us to move there. But Carolyn was adamant. "Anywhere but there," she said. "I've followed you to Australia and I'll live in a tent in the Maine woods if you like, but don't make me go to California." She had an irrational aversion to Californians with their permanent tans and their Have a Nice Days. I wheedled and coaxed, but she wasn't buying.

"Look," I said. "I'm spending more and more time in L.A. It's where my work is. Let's just go and rent an empty house and camp out in it for a while. If you still hate California in a few months, I promise you we'll move back east."

Eventually, as I knew I would (as I always did), I wore her down. Once she'd accepted the idea in principle, I talked her into flying out there with me (just to look around), and we wound up buying a house in Pacifici Palisades. Then we sold the Miami apartment and had our furniture shipped west. That's the way things worked with us. I got what I wanted and she plunged in and seemed to become happy about it.

We sold our beautiful little beach house, too. I don't think she ever forgave me for insisting we get rid of it. Looking back, I find it hard to forgive myself. Our happiest days were spent there.

It was late June and we set out to cross the country in our new van. The old '61 van had died on a highway in Florida one day the year before. What it had actually done, bless its heart, was to grind down to five miles an hour . . . and manage to carry us to a VW dealership in the next town. There, we told the salesman that if he could call our New York bank and arrange financing within an hour's time, we'd buy a new van from him. He did and we did. Years later, someone told me that he had been in that same VW dealership, heard the story and been told that our old van had been put up on blocks and become someone's greenhouse.

Six of us and a pet cat we'd acquired, named Trisky (for our lucky number 13), were California bound. We took a leisurely two weeks to cross the country, stopping when we felt like it. We'd drive far into the night, letting the kids doze in the van, curled up in their sleeping bags. Trisky slept on the dashboard in front of the steering wheel. When we got tired, we'd pull over and check in to a Holiday Inn, sleep as late as we wanted, and then start out again.

I loved the quiet hours at night best, with Carolyn beside me, the rest of the family asleep and the cat purring on the dashboard. One night, she escaped out a motel window and we thought we'd seen the last of her, but in the morning she was back. From then on, we let her out the window of each motel we stayed in and she always returned.

On July 1st we plunged into the Mohave on the last leg of our trip. The heat was almost unendurable. The van's air conditioner could only be run for five minutes at a time before it started pumping air that was even hotter than that outside. We thought the cat was dying. She lay on the dashboard panting and rolling her eyes. But the remarkable creature survived and so did we, and we all emerged at last into the green hills and valleys of Southern California.

X

I haven't been able to figure out why I feel so scared all the time lately. I wake up scared, spend most of the day scared and go to bed scared. So when I hear there's something which will conquer fear in one three-hour session, of course I decide to try it. I send in my fifty bucks and on the appointed night I hop in my car and drive to the Pacific Palisades Camp Grounds. It's only a half hour away.

The guy in charge is named Tolly Burkan and it is he who will teach us how to walk on fire. There are forty would-be California fakirs in the group, crammed into a room in a small, ramshackle building on a hill. After we have settled down and been given disclaimers to sign, acquitting the management of all responsibility for ruined pedal extremities, our guru for the evening leads us outside. It's 7:45 P.M., a clear winter night, California cashmere weather.

At the bottom of the hill, we come to a large pile of railroad ties cut into four-foot lengths. "Everybody grab one and we'll show you what to do." Burkan and his helpers demonstrate the correct way of stacking wood to make a bonfire. Then they pour kerosine over the huge formation, apply a match and flames light up the night sky.

Back up the hill we climb to our classroom. It will take three and a half hours for the fire to cook down to a bed of hot coals. While we wait, white-knuckled and nervously giggling, Tolly Burkan gives us his pitch. It's the usual New Age stuff: mind over matter. ("I don't mind and you don't matter." Billy Garrigan's old one-liner pops into my head.)

"There are three rules you have to remember," Tolly says. "Pay attention. Expect the best. And go for it." I've heard variations on the theme before, but this time I'm listening in a different context: we are going to walk on fire tonight . . . or else, we're going to chicken out. Either choice will be traumatic.

"People have been doing this for centuries," says Tolly Burkan, "and frankly, no one really knows how or why it works." Our group is not here to learn the parlor trick of fire walking, he explains. Letting go of arbitrary fear is what we need to learn. And all fear, he claims, is arbitrary. "If you can overcome your apprehension tonight, the fire will not burn you. If you can't let go of fear, you dare not take the walk." I think of African tribes I've read about, where a suspected felon's guilt or innocence is determined by plunging his hand into boiling water. The innocent feel nothing; the guilty are scalded.

"Imagine the worst possible scenario," says our teacher, "and decide if you can live with it." The smell of scorching flesh pervades the nostrils of my imagination. "Oh well," I tell myself, "I can always become a stump dancer." The real scent of roasting railroad ties wafts through the half-open window. "Am I actually going through with this? Schmuck. Why? What for?" But I know the answer. I'm so damned sick of feeling afraid. I know my fear is self-imposed. I know I have nothing to be scared of. And I know I have to give up fear, at least for tonight, if I intend to take this walk.

At 10:15 P.M. we troop back down the hill. The night air is chillier now, but a number of us are sweating. We approach the fire. "Please take off your shoes and socks and roll up your pants if you're wearing them. Please do this whether you plan to take the walk or not." We obey obediently: ("You will be given bars of soap. Do not be alarmed; these rooms contain only showers."). We find safe places for our belongings, then join hands, making a great ring around the fire. Burkin's assistants appear with heavy rakes and pitchforks. They are wearing combat boots. Using their implements, they rake the dying bonfire into a path about five feet wide and nine feet long.

We are standing a dozen feet away and the heat is so intense we can hardly bear it. "This is lunacy," I tell myself. "It's cuckoo time. I've done a lot of crazy things in my life . . . etc., etc., blah, blah, blah . . ." The roof chatter goes on and on. Ol' debil Ego is in a state of panic.

"The temperature in the fire bed is approximately 1100 degrees," says Tolly Burkan. "Aluminum liquifies at this temperature and can be poured into castings." I glance at the guy whose right hand I am holding. He looks as scared as I am. "There's no shame in deciding not to take the walk," Tally continues. My ego is going bonkers. He doesn't want Orson to look like a wimp any more than I do. But he senses there's nothing in it for him if we take this trip.

"Remember the three rules," says Tolly Burkan. "One. Pay attention: my assistants will walk first and you'll see that they're not getting burned. Two. Expect the best: decide you're going to accomplish what you intend to do. And finally, rule number three. Go for it: step onto these coals and walk. Don't go too fast or you might trip and fall down. And whatever you do, don't stop. If you do, you will burn."

Burkan disappears into the circle and there's a moment of silence. The heat is intense. I stare down at the vivid swath. Flames are dancing around the glowing coals.

Suddenly a man, one of Burkan's assistants, steps from the ring of people, moves across the small buffer zone of grass and walks onto the red-hot coal bed. I hold my breath, watching him with fascination. His feet are sinking into the coals. Flames shoot up around him. He takes four or five steps across the length of the path and then he is off, stomping up and down in a damp patch of grass. My heart is pounding.

Now another man walks out into the inferno, and following him, a woman. She is wearing a dress and clutches her skirt up around her thighs. People are now walking in a steady flow across the nine-foot length of fire. I see it; I experience it; I don't believe it. "I can't do this," my ego screams inside my head. "OK pal," I answer. "You stay here. I'm leaving. Everything's going to be hunky-dory." I'm not afraid now. I let go of my partners' hands and move toward the fire. When an opening presents itself, I step out onto the burning coals. The heat is intense. I feel the hardness of the burning embers under my soles. My feet have always been tender. It occurs to me that when I was a Boy Scout, I never rose above the rank of Tenderfoot. I look down. Little tongues of flames are licking between my toes. As I take each step, disturbing the fire bed, dozens of tiny broiling embers dance onto my feet.

I walk at a deliberate, moderately slow pace, determined not to rush the experience. Four steps, five, and now I'm off into the cool grass, elated, victorious, my heart leaping for joy. My feet have not burned. There are still embers on them. I hop up and down in the dewey grass, dislodging the burning remnants. I can't keep the grin off my face. Somewhere inside, my ego is sulking. "Big deal. Who gives a shit? It's probably a trick." People are pumping my hand and congratulating me. I am grinning like John Henry Faulk's egg-sucking dawg. I feel such pride. It's a pride that doesn't seem to be connected with my poor, miserable ego.

By the end of the firewalk, 31 of the 40 enrollees have taken the trip. There is a euphoria among the walkers.

People are clapping one another on the back. I spot one of the guys who didn't walk. He seems depressed. I hear him say to one of the other non-participants, "I really just came to observe."

The next day, as fate would have it, I am booked on one of my infrequent television appearances. I am to tape five half-hour *Super Password* shows for NBC. During the third program, I find myself in the big money Bonus Game, sitting opposite an excited contestant. If I can come up with clues that help her find ten secret words in 60 seconds, she will win $45,000. With the prize money that high, tension mounts. I remind myself to PAY ATTENTION (to the words for which I need to find clues . . . and to my partner's responses), EXPECT THE BEST (This is an easy game if the players are relaxed), and GO FOR IT (The buzzer sounds). Effortlessly, one after another, I give the right clues. Thirty-three seconds later the contestant is screaming, jumping up and down and hugging Bert Convy, the host of the show.

Life isn't frightening. Life is a Game Show where people who have fun are the winners. If I can just remember this, I'll be Home free. But *You Know Who* is always at work, reminding me to hold on to my Worry franchise. What if? What if? What if?

What if Carolyn really hates California?

Venice, California, 1987

XI

We had bought a house in Pacific Palisades (technically, part of L.A.) because it reminded us of the east. Real deciduous trees lined its streets, along with year 'round California bloomers. An actor friend of ours from back home lived there and had touted us onto the place.

The new house was wonderful. Even Carolyn came to love it. On the street in front of it were kids on bicycles and neighbors washing their cars. But go through the place and on into the back yard and you were in Shangri La. Except for an occasional plane passing overhead, it was totally private; we could go skinny dipping in the pool. The view was of the blue Pacific and Catalina Island. Ringing the property were huge eucalyptus trees. The Palisades was full of them; they'd originally been imported from Australia.

We had a big fireplace in the living room. Sliding glass doors led into the back yard. Our bedroom had a fireplace too, and its own door to the back yard, so I could wake up each morning and stumble right into the pool.

Carolyn hung dozens of plants in the windows of the

kitchen, and from its ceiling. She couldn't make up her mind what to put on the floor. "I'm sick of tile and linoleum," she said. Finally, she decided to have some fun and told the carpet man to install Astroturf. Our kitchen-garden was absurd and wonderful. When crumbs fell, they disappeared into the grass. Once a week I'd vacuum them out.

The living room had beautifully polished wood floors like those of a New England farm house. We placed plants and potted trees everywhere. The furniture arrived, having travelled from New York to Sydney to Miami to California. Our paintings covered every inch of wall space. For the first time in years, the children would have their own individual bedrooms. Still, Zeke and Max chose to share a room, and they all continued to sleep in groups. The nesting habits they'd learned on the road were hard to break.

The canyon behind our house was teeming with life. At night, we could hear coyotes howling in it. They'd been driven unnaturally close to civilization that year by a shortage of their regular diet, which consisted of small rodents. I read this in the paper at the time, but don't remember the details. What I do remember is seeing pairs of coyotes streak across the streets at night, caught in the glare of our car's headlights, their eyes iridescent. It was an eerie sight.

Our beautiful cat Trisky, after surviving the cross-country trip in the van, became dinner for one of them, less than a week after we'd arrived. We were all grief stricken, and no one thought of replacing her for quite a while. We needed a period of time to mourn the passing of a family member. But when a few months had gone by, the children began asking if we could have another cat. Susie wanted a dog, but was overruled. Oddly enough, every cat we ever owned was attracted to Susie, choosing to sleep with her, making her room its home. Natural feline perversity, perhaps.

One day, we all piled into the van and headed for the

animal shelter to make an adoption. We had decided to look for a young adult cat. All kittens are adorable; not many grown cats are. The only way to tell what you're going to be living with for years is to choose one whose personality is already formed.

At the Santa Monica Animal Shelter, in the last cage on the left, was a four-fifths-grown gray, female, domestic short hair, who almost literally spoke to us. We fell in love at once and asked if we could have her. "Come back in five days," said the man in charge. "They have to stay here for a week to have their immunity shots. We open at eight A.M. If you're here first, you get her."

The fifth day was Halloween. The kids were in their costumes for the school party. When our van pulled up in front of the shelter at 7:55 A.M., there were a dozen people waiting to get in. It turned out they all wanted our gray girl. The fickle thing had turned her charms on to every potential adopter all week. "I've never seen anything like it," said the manager. "We'll have to be fair about this. We'll hold an auction and give her to the highest bidder."

"I don't want to be fair," whined Max. "I want our cat." Zeke began to cry.

"Cry louder," I whispered, poking him. "All of you start crying. Come on, damn it. Do what I tell you." A din arose, a clatter, a cacaphony . . . four children in Mickey Mouse suits and princess costumes sobbing loudly.

"Oh Christ," I heard someone mutter. "We can't fight that. Let them have her. We'll take one of the others."

We named the gray cat Sarah because she seemed somehow old fashioned. When in a few months she came into heat (we'd decided she should have the experience one time of being a mother), she proved she was decidedly modern, letting herself be courted by two toms at the same time. One was a three-legged yellow brute from up the street, the other the black-and-white tiger from next door.

"Oh, Sarah," sighed Michele. "What a decision. Which one are you going to let be the father of your kittens?"

When the litter was born, at the bottom of Susie's bed, two of the kittens were bright yellow, the remaining three had black and white stripes.

"I guess you couldn't decide, eh Sarah?" Max, the imp, was delighted.

"Well, it is California," said his mother.

We gave the kittens away, exhausting our new supply of friends in the process, and then had Sarah fixed. But the experience of motherhood had activated other of her instincts and she became (and remains to this day) a dedicated hunter, bringing a continual supply of expired or expiring wildlife into the house.

One morning we walked out the front door and saw Sarah sitting at the base of a tiny sapling we'd planted there not long before. She was staring fixedly at the top of it, where a terrified mouse clung. The baby tree was too slender and fragile to support the cat. As we watched, she tried several times to climb it, falling off each time, as the mouse swayed desperately back and forth like a flag pole sitter on a flexible pole.

There was no place for the mouse to run to if it jumped. The sapling was planted in a patch of earth surrounded by a brick patio floor, itself enclosed by a three-foot high brick wall. Sarah had the mouse trapped. It could stay where it was till exhaustion knocked it off. Sarah was content to wait. The cat-and-mouse game was on.

"God, sometimes nature's ugly," I said.

"That's your view of it," said Carolyn.

"What are we going to do?"

"Nothing. It's their business."

The children clamored, yelling and carrying on, but it was time for them to run to catch their bus for school. When they came home at four o'clock, the stalemate was still in effect. Sarah and the mouse were staring into each other's eyes.

"Oh God," the children howled. "Do something. Bad Sarah! Bad cat! Leave the poor little mouse alone."

"Jesus, I can't live with this," I said. "I've got to rescue the mouse."

"I think you should stay out of it," said Carolyn.

Susie whirled on her mother. "How can you be so cruel? I hate you and I hate Sarah." She stormed into her room and slammed the door. Zeke began to cry.

"All right," I said. "I'm going to take charge. I'm the man of the house. I should have some say in what goes on here." Going to my tool drawer, I dug out my work gloves and put them on. I walked to the front door, followed by Zeke, Max, Michele and Carolyn. I saw Susie watching from her bedroom window. For some reason, I was frightened of the mouse, afraid to touch it. I don't know why. But I managed to remain outwardly calm.

Sarah saw me coming, sensed my purpose. She got up and paced, her tail twitching furiously. I approached the mouse. Its beady eyes stared at me. I reached toward it. Frantically it jumped from its perch to another tiny branch. Sarah waited hungrily below.

"Jesus," I muttered. I needed to be firm, to simply reach out and grab the mouse. I was sweating, afraid to touch the poor cowering thing, afraid it would die in my hand or bite me or climb inside my shirt or down my pants. I didn't know what I was afraid of. I reached again and this time was able to grab it. The children roared with approval. I was afraid to hold it too tightly for fear of crushing it. It began to wriggle through my fingers. I pulled it to my chest, hoping to cradle it. It clutched at my shirt with its little claws and began to crawl onto me. I shrieked a high, falsetto shriek like ladies-in-movies-standing-on-chairs-to-escape-mice shriek.

"Eeek." The sound rang humiliatingly in my ears. I involuntarily let go of the mouse. It leapt heroically, landing almost directly next to Sarah, then sped past her and to refuge behind a large bush by the front of the house. It was now trapped in a corner between the house and the brick patio wall.

"God, Dad, what did you drop it for?" said Zeke. Carolyn rolled her eyes and went back into the house. A moment later, she reappeared, carrying a red plastic mop bucket and an 18-inch square piece of corrugated cardboard from a wine carton.

"This looks like a job for CarolynMan," she said. She motioned us all away from the corner where the mouse was trapped. The cat eyed her suspiciously.

"Sorry, Sarah," she said. Swiftly, she dropped the plastic pail over the mouse, which ran around inside it frantically. Then she slipped the cardboard under it, completing its capture.

"OK," she said to me. "Come here and put your foot on the bucket. The rest of you go into the house and close all the doors and windows." Sarah was going crazy, desperate to get at her mouse. The children ran inside, then returned a few minutes later to report that their work was done.

"Now," said Carolyn. "Slide your hand under the cardboard, keep your other hand on top of the bucket and bring mousie into the house. Kids, keep Sarah out here." I followed her orders, happy to be told what to do. I could feel the mouse scratching his way through the corrugated board, to get at my hand, to eat a hole through it, for all I knew. Carolyn held open the sliding glass door to the back yard and told me to carry my package through it. She slid the panel shut, then yelled to the children out front. "Let Sarah in and close the door behind her." In a flash, Sarah was there, glaring murderously through the glass door at me, scratching and clawing. Carolyn called to me through the glass. "Take him down the canyon and let him go."

Gingerly, I climbed through a hole in the hedge at the back end of the yard. Then I clambered down about fifteen feet and lifted the pail up from its cardboard floor. The mouse leaped out and disappeared in the underbrush. Wearily, I climbed back.

"Be careful," Carolyn called from inside. "Come in the kitchen door, otherwise Sarah will get out." I slipped quickly into the kitchen.

"Jesus," I said. "Make me a drink."

The cat was wild with rage. She raced through the

house, going from door to door, caterwauling her fury
and disappointment. A quarter of an hour went by, the
kids retreated to the TV room to catch the Flintstones,
and I sat in the kitchen watching Carolyn prepare our
dinner. All at once, I became aware of a new sound from
Sarah, out in the living room at the sliding glass door. It
was a low, moaning growl.

"Now what?" I muttered. I got up, carrying my drink,
and went to see what was wrong. When I got to the living room what I saw astonished me. There was Sarah,
lying flat, nose pressed up against the glass door, tail
twitching, low sound rumbling out of her throat. On the
other side of the door, looking in, sat the mouse.

"You're not going to believe this, honey, but come in
here!"

She hurried out of the kitchen, followed by the children, who'd heard me calling to her. When they saw it,
they all gasped.

"You couldn't have put him very far down the canyon,"
said Michele.

"I didn't think I had to."

"He must have gotten confused," said Susie.

"He doesn't look confused to me," said Carolyn. "He
looks like he knows exactly what he wants, and that's
Sarah."

"Oh, God," I moaned. "Get the bucket and catch him
again. This time I'll take him all the way down."

"All right, but this is the last time. If he comes back
again, I'm letting Sarah have him."

"All right, all right. Just get the pail."

Superwife repeated her rescue effort and once again, I
began the steep descent into the canyon, going all the way
down this time, catching my pants on brambles, slipping
and sliding on loose shale. Almost a hundred and fifty feet
down, I lifted the pail once more, and out went mouse.
Up I labored then, until, covered with burrs, scrapes and
scratches, I arrived in the kitchen again.

Sarah, more furious than ever, tore along the walls,
sinking her claws into the wallpaper.

"God what a day. Where's my drink? When's dinner going to be ready?"

It took half an hour this time for the mouse to come back, crawling exhausted up to the patio door and lying down in front of her tormentor.

"That's it. I'm letting Sarah out. All right? Agreed?"

"Yes."

"Yeah."

"Yes."

"Yes, Mom."

"OK."

She slid the door open. Up jumped the mouse and ran, pursued by the cat, which caught it, swiped at it with its paw and sent it crashing up against the side of the house. I closed the door and went back into the kitchen, shaking my head with wonder.

"Look," said Carolyn. "You read me bits out of that book of interviews with people who'd been pronounced clinically dead. They all said dying was a beautiful experience, and some of them hated it when they felt themselves being brought back to life. They fought like crazy to go back down that tunnel or whatever it was they saw. It's obvious that when that mouse realized there was no way out of that little tree except into Sarah's mouth, at some point he accepted it. And you interfered with the process."

"I just can't believe it. I just can't believe it."

"Trust the process, honey. That's what you always tell me. Trust the process."

"When's dinner?"

We had occasion to travel to Phoenix in our stalwart van. The city was 400 miles away, through the hated Mohave, but the invitation was from friends we really cared about. We made it there, spent a festive weekend and then, on Sunday morning, headed back.

About two hours into the desert, the van's engine suddenly began making a noise from the sound track of a Japanese horror movie. Then it ground to a halt, several miles from the nearest cactus. I got out, opened the back panel and stared at the engine for a while. This having exhausted my mechanical expertise, a family conference was called. We decided that Carolyn and the kids would stay with the car, while I hitchhiked to the next town for help.

I walked a few yards up the highway and peered in the direction of Phoenix. Nothing was coming. What looked like a vulture circled overhead. After ten minutes, a car appeared on the horizon. As it approached, it slowed down and I could see that the driver was checking out the situation: stalled van, wife and kids sitting on a rock in the morning sun, hapless husband going for assistance. The car speeded up and zoomed past me. I glanced over at Carolyn. A running argument between us had concerned her unwillingness to pick up hitchhikers versus my basic decency. She had the grace to lower her eyes.

Finally a car stopped. The driver (as he subsequently told me in an endless monologue) turned out to be a private eye, working for an insurance company. He was on his way back to L.A. after five days in Phoenix, shadowing a guy through a couple of motels and taking secret movies of him. When the guy showed up in court six weeks later, sporting a neck brace and an aluminum walker, he'd be treated to full color movies of himself diving into the Holiday Inn pool and buying drinks for a young woman in a one-piece bathing suit.

The private eye wasn't sure how far away the next town was, but after five days on the road, he was happy for the company. Fifty miles later, we came to Quartzite. It had three gas stations (and not much less) but no tow truck.

Thirty miles farther along, we arrived in the sizeable desert municipality of Blythe. I thanked the gumshoe, bid him goodbye and started looking for a tow truck. It was Sunday and only one was operating, at the Gulf station next to McDonald's. The driver was out on call but would be back in "a few minutes." He returned three hours later, agreed to accept my $150, and we were on our way

back down the highway in his tow truck. I'd been gone a
long time by then, and *National Enquirer* headlines kept
flashing through my mind: ACTOR'S FAMILY DECIMATED BY
DESERT WEIRDOS.

Our van appeared on the horizon and I was sure I
could make out survivors. The desert, with the late afternoon sun casting long shadows, was breathtakingly prehistoric. The tow truck arrived and the family hungrily polished off the Big Macs I'd brought for them. The vehicles
achieved dockage and, with the van's front wheels up in
the air, lumbered off like two gargantuan dogs in heat,
humping along the highway.

The kids stayed in the van; Carolyn and I rode in the
cab with the driver. She recounted the adventures she'd
had while I was gone: the desert isolation, peaceful at
first, the children discovering that ants like Captain
Crunch better than Cheerios. Never a cop all day, of
course. And then the dreaded arrival of Charles Manson.
A guy, she said, had pulled up in a battered Chevy with
Florida plates. He'd had long, greasy hair, a missing front
tooth and a T-shirt with a picture of a drunken cat in a
champagne glass. The legend under the picture read HAPPI-
NESS IS A TIGHT PUSSY. Glancing down at her four kids,
Carolyn had sighed with relief and thought, "Thank God
that leaves me out."

But the guy's appearance had been deceptive; he'd
turned out to be decent and helpful. After spending half
an hour under the car, he'd crawled back out and apolo-
gized.

"I'm sorry, lady, but there's nothin' I can do. Your
valves are shot." (I wasn't surprised, we'd had trouble
with them from the beginning.) "Whatever you do," said
the guy, "don't let them fix the car in the desert. Pay the
money and have it towed to L.A."

But Know-It-All here had spotted a VW dealership in
Blythe, while waiting for the tow truck. We had the van
dropped off there and checked into the motel across the
street, where we spent the night fooling with the vertical
hold on the TV. In the morning, I walked over and spoke

to the people at VW. They confirmed what Happiness-Is-a-Tight-Pussy had said about the valves but challenged his idea that they should not be allowed to fix the car. "It's a $600 job," they said, "but you're in luck. Even though you're out of warranty" (I was, of course, *just*). "Volkswagon will probably pick up two-thirds of the tab because of all the valve problems you've had in the past." They advised us to go home, and assured us we'd be hearing from them in a few days.

We rented a car, collected our stuff from the motel and took off at seventy miles an hour through the empty desert. Instantly there appeared behind us the cop who hadn't been there all day yesterday. License, registration, $50 ticket, "Have a nice day."

Two mornings later, the good news came by phone. The dealership in Blythe said that VW would do the decent thing and pick up two-thirds of the damage, so I'd only be out $200 (in addition, of course, to the $150 for towing, the tab for the motel, the $65 to Hertz for a car to drive home and the rented wheels while our van was being fixed). We told them to go ahead. The car would be ready on Friday and the service manager, for a modest fee, would deliver it to our door. Not bad.

Friday came and went and then another Friday and still a third. I screamed, I pulled my hair, I howled into the phone. The Blythe people turned sullen and then hostile. At last they called to announce that, the correct parts finally having arrived from Stuttgart or wherever, the van would be delivered to me the next morning by a mechanic who was coming to L.A. to spend the weekend. I sighed with relief and then heard the caller say, "Please have a certified check for $611.10 ready."

My jaw dropped. "But you said VW would pick up two-thirds of the bill."

"You must be mistaken, sir. We never said that. Your car is out of warranty."

"But you said . . ."

"Mr. Bean, if you want the vehicle, have a certified check ready for our man."

"All right. Send the van. I'll have the check ready." I gnashed my teeth, I rolled my eyes, I uttered curses. Then, I sat quietly, thinking. How could I avoid becoming the shaftee in this matter? I suddenly remembered a Peter Maas article I'd read years before, about gypsies. An evil smile crept over my face and I decided on a plan.

When the delivery man from Blythe showed up with my van the next day, I had a sealed envelope addressed to the dealer. In it was a blank piece of paper. I had placed this envelope under a book, which I held in my hand as I walked out to the driveway. On top of the book was a duplicate envelope, unsealed, with a certified check for $611.10 in it. I showed the check to the grease monkey, sealed it in the envelope, looked him in the eye and admonished him to deliver it personally to his employer.

"You can count on me, Mr. Bean." His eyes looked directly into mine to show his earnestness, and at that moment I pulled the old Gypsy switch and handed him the envelope from under the book, the one with the blank piece of paper in it.

"Put this in your pocket," I said, "and see that your boss gets it first thing Monday morning." The poor boob wished me a nice weekend and drove off with his empty envelope.

Carolyn, peering from the window, saw me dance a terrible David Merrick jig in the driveway. I was still out a lot of dough, of course, and I knew I'd have to settle with the pirates from Blythe eventually. But at least I was now in a position to bargain. Looking back on our night in the desert, I realized we were lucky they hadn't sold the lot of us into slavery.

Two hours later, the phone rang. It was the guy who had delivered the van. Curiosity apparently having gotten the better of him, he had opened the envelope and discovered the blank piece of paper. "What the hell are you trying to do to me," he screamed.

"It's not my fault, man," I said. "The check had a curse on it. The envelope shouldn't have been opened until Monday."

I wound up paying the $200 I'd originally been quoted. It turned out that Blythe was collecting from the parent company and then trying to charge me, too. At least, that's what I deduced from the answer I received after writing to the president of Volkswagen of America.

Carolyn came up with a moral to the story: If a greasy haired guy in a HAPPINESS IS A TIGHT PUSSY T-shirt ever offers you advice, for God's sake, do what the man says.

Little Zeke could not swim. He had lived around water all his life and loved it. In the pool at Miami or the ocean at Westhampton, he had splashed and played with Max, Susie and Michele, but always under the necessarily watchful eye of his mother. At the Palm Bay Club, Carolyn had found two female swimming instructors named Blondie and Marie. They were optimistic about our little boy's potential. "He's less than a year old. Now is the time of his least resistance." Blondie and Marie were wrong. They would toss Zeke into the pool and he would sink to the bottom of it and just sit there. After several weeks, they finally gave up. "He refuses to learn, Mrs. Bean."

Now we were living in California with a pool in our own back yard.

"He simply has to become a swimmer," said Carolyn, "or I'm going to be a nervous wreck all the time." The YMCA operated an emormous pool in the foothills overlooking Pacific Palisades. They offered daily classes for beginning swimmers. These were to commence the week we arrived in town. Zeke was then three years old.

On the first day, I drove him up the hill to the giant facility.

"You're going to learn to swim, boy," I told him. He shook his head.

"No," he said. "I'm not."

Each and every week day of the summer of '74, Carolyn or I sat for an hour beside the YMCA pool. Toddlers came and toddlers went. They cried, they splashed, they swallowed water, they coughed . . . and ultimately, they learned to swim. Zeke did not.

"I've never seen anyone as stubborn in my life," said the pool director. "Bring him back next year and we'll try again. He'll be a year older. Maybe he'll learn then."

"No," said Zeke. "I won't."

I spoke to Carolyn: "Honey, why don't you stop worrying about him. He wears his little yellow inflatable arm floats and he can't drown with those on. And besides, Susie or Max or Michele are always with him."

"But they can't be watching him every minute. And sometimes he plays around the pool when he's not even swimming. What if he fell in and hit his head and no one even knew about it?"

"What if the Goodyear blimp fell out of the sky and landed on him? You can't cover every possibility."

She was not to be placated: "I want to hire someone to come and give him private lessons here in his own back yard. Maybe he was embarrassed in front of all those other kids."

"Do what you have to do. But it's just possible that there's no solution."

Carolyn called the Y. Yes, they could recommend a man for the job. He lived nearby in Santa Monica and was a certified swimming instructor.

The next afternoon at 3:00 o'clock, a Honda 750 motorcycle pulled into our driveway. A well-built young man in his early twenties dismounted and rang our doorbell. In the children's playroom, Zeke did not look up from the cartoon he was watching on TV. Carolyn answered the door.

"Hello," said the young man. "My name is Bob Miller." Carolyn called Zeke. He walked slowly out of the playroom, wearing his baggy bathing trunks.

"Hi there," said Bob Miller. "Are you ready to learn how to swim?"

"No," answered Zeke. Bob Miller lasted three weeks as Zeke's swimming instruction. (But more about him later.)

Spring of '75 came to the Palisades, and Carolyn began talking about enrolling Zeke in the daily classes again.

"Do what you want," I told her. "But leave me out of

it. I'm not spending another summer sitting beside the YMCA pool. I'm through worrying about him. If he wants to drown himself, it's his business."

"How can you talk so callously about your own son?"

"I'm not being callous; I'm being loving. It's no favor to the boy to try to take responsibility for him. He's got to learn to do that for himself. Anyway, I think he's doing a big number on us, getting all this attention and concern and money lavished on him. Jesus, our whole lives are revolving around teaching Zeke to swim."

"Well, he still has to learn to swim if we're going to live with a pool."

"What he has to learn is to take responsibility for himself. Anyway . . ." I looked around to make sure our son was not within earshot. "I think the little so-and-so knows how to swim already. If we stop making such a big deal of all this, he'll be paddling around like Mark Spitz."

"Can you be sure of that, Orson?"

"Not 100 percent sure, no. But sure enough that I'm willing to take the chance . . . for his sake, for our sake, for everyone's sake. We can't go on like this."

Carolyn chewed her lip nervously.

"I don't know," she said. "I just don't know. I'll have to sleep on it." The next day I brought the subject up again . . . and the day after that . . . and finally, she agreed. We would sit our son down and have a talk with him.

The children were out of school for the long Memorial Day weekend. Zeke was at the pool, sitting on the edge of it, inflated yellow plastic floats on his upper arms, his feet dangling in the water. Max and Susie were splashing and laughing. I called to him from the kitchen.

"What do you want, Dad?" he yelled back.

"Come in here. Your mom and I want to talk to you."

"What about?"

"Just come in here a minute." He slowly crept to the kitchen door.

"Dry your feet off before you come in." Carolyn handed him a frayed towel from the hook next to the sink.

"Can I have a can of Coke?"

"May I have a can of Coke. Yes." The amenities attended to, the three of us sat staring stonily at one another around the kitchen table. Then Carolyn indicated with a nod of her head that I should begin.

"Well, Zekie," I said. "Your mom and I want you to know that we are never going to make you take another swimming lesson." His eyes narrowed with suspicion. He glanced over his shoulder and out the kitchen window at his brother and sister.

"Do I still get to play in the pool?"

"Yes. You can do anything you want. You can wear your rubber arm things or leave them off. If you fall in the pool and drown and your mother and I don't have our sweet Zekie any more, we'll be very sad and we'll cry a lot . . . but it's your business. We're through hassling you about it. Anyway, I think you already know how to swim. I think all kids are born knowing how to swim and remember it when they see their older brothers and sisters swimming. But whether you swim or not is your business." There was a long pause during which Zeke looked at his can of Coke. He took a drink from it, then spoke.

"Can I go now?"

"May I go now. Yes."

For the rest of the day, he stayed away from the pool. The next day he sat at the edge of it, dangling his feet, looking up at the kitchen window occasionally to see if his mother was watching him. On the morning of day three, he was in the water, and that afternoon he swam from one side of the pool to the other. Whoops of joy and congratulations rose up from the mouths of Max, Susie and Michele. Carolyn started out through the kitchen door.

"For God's sake, stay in here," I cried, stopping her just in time. Her eyes looked momentarily hurt, then she relaxed and smiled. I walked over to her and took her in my arms.

"We have to act like we don't notice anything. Later on we can have a celebration and burn the water wings."

He swam for the rest of the day like a California catfish, and the subject of pool safety never came up in our house again. We were starting to trust the process.

In Los Angeles we were surrounded by people who took care of their bodies. To these Californians, everything edible represented a potential hazard. Entertaining them was not easy. When Carolyn would phone to invite our new friends to dinner, the vegetarians among them would have to be assured that they'd be served salad or pasta. There were veggies within concentric circles of veggies. Some ate only certain kinds of pasta. For them, there had to be noodles made of spinach or of some other green substance.

One couple brought their own set of pots and pans to our house. They'd purchased them through the mail from a Spiritually Enlightened Culinary Master in Japan. The couple stayed in the kitchen as Carolyn prepared dinner, working next to her, cooking their own separate meal in the spiritual pots. What they made looked like seaweed and they ate it glumly at the dinner table, seeming not even to want to look at the bad stuff the rest of us were putting into our mouths.

Once, as a joke, we served Hostess Twinkies, Drake's Yankee Doodles and Devil Dogs for dessert. "Pure pleasure," we told our guests. "No known nutrient." The spinach noodle people were not amused.

"Do you know," said one of them, "that the BHT in the cellophane wrapper of these so-called cakes has been found to cause cancer in laboratory animals?"

"There was an experiment which was hushed up," I answered, "in which white rats were forced to listen to tapes of Ralph Nader speeches, and the rats developed cancer." No one laughed.

Later on that evening, we passed around a joint of Maui Wowie. After smoking it, two of the health food addicts fell on the Twinkies and devoured them voraciously, crying. "I don't care! I don't care!"

When my grandfather was ninety, he went to a doctor

for his annual checkup. The doctor said he should stop smoking his cigars. Shortly before he died at the age of ninety-seven, he told me that one of his major regrets in life was having listened to that doctor when he was ninety. I decided to learn from my grandfather's experience and stop worrying about my health. Whatever else may or may not cause illness, worry attracts it.

Professional muggers in New York have said in interviews that they watch the way people walk in the streets. Apprehensive, nervous, "victim" types are the ones they pick out to mug. They don't regard self-assured walkers as potential clients. Viruses and germs must operate the same way. During the Black Plague in Europe, certain people were too *busy* to get sick. Somebody had to keep things going, to pile up the stiffs on the sidewalk every morning so they could be collected.

My attitude began to change. I stopped "catching" colds, threw my catcher's mitt away and let the viruses float by and settle on someone else. My back, which had used to bother me from time to time, stopped doing so.

Max, at the age of eight, had his own cross to bear. A good-looking boy, he had been afflicted for years with warts. He had a giant "planter's wart" on the palm of his right hand, and literally hundreds of small "satellite warts" running up his arm. At different times in different cities and towns where we'd lived, we'd had the main wart burned off, frozen off or chemically treated by dermatologists. After each treatment, the wart came back. I decided that dermatologists ought to work with a mask and rattle. Dancing in circles around their patients would help more than most of the cures I've ever seen them attempt.

Max had to go into the hospital for minor surgery on a hernia. Since he was to be put to sleep with a general anesthetic, we suggested to the surgeon that the wart be cut out, too. He agreed. When the operation was over, he said to us, "I removed the entire wart and enough of the surrounding tissue that it can never return."

The wart was back in a week. I'd had enough. I said to Max, "You know, I think you like having that wart."

"I don't," he protested.

"I think you do. It gets you lots of attention, and your mom and I have to worry about it and spend lots of money trying to get rid of it. Well, I want you to know that I'm through worrying about it and I'm never going to spend another cent on it. It's your wart and you can have it and learn to love it or you can decide to get rid of it."

"How can I get rid of it if the doctors can't?" he wailed.

"Here," I said, handing him a piece of white typewriter paper. "Draw the outline of your hand on this. Make a mark where the wart is. Then burn the paper and the wart will disappear."

"That's ridiculous," he said. "Give me a break."

"This is an old secret cure, known to the Druids. It will work if you want it to." He stormed out of the room.

A few weeks later, Carolyn and I were sitting on the living room floor in front of our fireplace. Max had received some severe badgering from Susie and Zeke about his "monster arm." He came into the room carrying a piece of paper. The outline of his hand and arm were on it. There was a circle on the palm and hundreds of dots up the arm. We pretended not to notice as he solemnly burned the paper. He looked as if he had made a decision.

The next day, the wart had become noticeably smaller. In a week, it was completely gone, along with the hundreds of warts which had lived on his arm for years and the scar which the surgeon's knife had left in his palm.

One of my appearances on *The Tonight Show* was coming up and when it did, I told the story. During the next few weeks, I received dozens of letters from people who had seen the show. They told about similar cures they'd effected on their own warts. I also got one angry letter, written on loose-leaf binder paper in pencil. "You have misled the public," it read. "A dumb thing like that won't help warts. You shouldn't give people useless and ignorant information. The only way to get rid of warts is to rub a quarter on them and then bury it."

Nineteen seventy-five turned into 1976, the year of the bicentennial, and across the country every village and town planned its own celebration. I got a phone call from Burlington, Vermont, one day. Sweet old Grandpa and my grandmother had lived there at the time of my birth, in a red brick house on Adams Street not far from the University of Vermont campus. My mother had been visiting her folks then, because my father was away doing a job in Tennessee or someplace. I never did get the exact story, though I asked about it on and off for years. Every kid is fascinated with the details of his own birth: the greatest story ever told. When I was twelve I did some math involving wedding dates, birth dates and numbers of anniversaries and came up with an uncheering conclusion. Math never did do me any good.

Burlington was a dull place for a kid to visit. This was my experience, though I loved my grandparents a lot. There was always a university scholarship student staying free in the spare attic room of their house. I never saw much of him because he left early to go to school and then worked evenings, putting himself through college. There were no other young people around and certainly no kids. The old lady next door (even my grandmother called her the old lady) would occasionally invite me over for melba toast (made in the oven) and cambric tea. Everything in her house had doilies on it. Even the old lady wore doilies, or what looked like doilies.

My grandfather had a wind-up Victrola in the den off the front parlor, and a 78 RPM collection that included such comedy classics as *The Two Black Crows* and *Gallagher and Sheehan*. I played them incessantly, rewinding the mechanism after each spin and replacing the needle with a new, sharp cactus point. They were my grandfather's favorites. When I was eight, I accidently broke the *Gallagher and Sheehan* record. Fifty years later I can still feel the sense of guilt, shame and loss.

My grandparents' house was filled with laughter. On a shelf in the parlor stood hardbound books of Sunday comic strips: *Buster Brown and His Dog Tige, Billy the Boy Artist* and best of all, the *Dreams of a Mince Pie Fiend*, which I found to be bizarre and wonderful. Today this strip is considered a work of comic genius: brilliantly drawn full-page layouts in which a mince pie addict, though warned by experience not to, overindulges in the forbidden substance before retiring and has, in his sleep, what would now be called hallucenogenic trips . . . shrinking to the size of an atom in one strip I recall and travelling through the inner workings of a trumpet. At the end of each episode, the poor fiend wakes up and swears off mince pie forever.

All of Burlington seemed to me to be constructed of the same dull red brick my grandparents' house was made of. "Four bricks thick," Grandpa would brag, speaking of the walls of his house. "Cool in the summer, warm in the winter." The town was a sleepy, homely one filled with old people (the memory of a very young boy). The tiny business district (my grandfather used to say, "Burlington has one Yellow Page.") consisted of Five and Tens and barber shops. There were, as I recall, two movie theaters, one of which had been placed off-limits by my grandmother, though I sometimes "snuck in" anyway. Years later, in the early fifties, I returned to Burlington and found myself standing in front of that same movie theater. The film showing was *Nature Girl and the Slave Trader*, a European soft core sex flick. The still pictures under the marquee showed a bare breasted French gamin of the Brigette Bardot variety, tied to a palm tree and being menaced by spear-carrying Africans. I was astonished. In those days nothing that sexually explicit was appearing in New York or, as far as I could see, anywhere else in the country. I asked a Burlingtonian the reason for such liberality.

"Vermont is one of the only states in the country, if not the only one," he said, "which allows no censorship of any kind. We don't like crappy movies like this playing downtown for the college kids to go see. But Ethan Allen didn't whip the British so that folks could tell other folks what they can or cannot do."

By the nineteen eighties, Burlington had become, of all things, the first American city to elect a Socialist mayor.

But this was 1976 and the phone call I received was from the head of Burlington's bicentennial committee, wanting to know if I'd consider flying there to become parade marshall for the big 4th of July celebration. I asked if they'd be able to pick up the tab for my wife and kids to come too. They grumbled a bit about the money, then agreed. Carolyn and I talked it over and decided we should go. "It's a sleepy little college town," I told her. "It'll be quiet, but fun for the kids. Two days of Norman Rockwell Americana."

On the 2nd of July we flew to Chicago and spent the night there with friends. The next morning they drove us to the airport and we caught a plane for Burlington. The kids didn't seem to mind that the big celebration with the Tall Ships would be in New York City. They were convinced that Burlington was the center of bicentennial activity. When we de-planed, we found a bus-load of people waiting to greet us. They cheered and pumped our hands. They carried signs which read WELCOME BEANS and WELCOME CAROLYN AND ORSON AND KIDS. Flashbulbs popped as a reporter from the Free Press jockied for pictures. I was the home town boy made good. Revellers surrounded our family. The children clung to us, overwhelmed by the attention. Each of them was handed clusters of red, white and blue balloons.

"C'mon Zekie. Susie take his hand. Max and Mimi, get aboard." Carolyn herded her brood on to the festive yellow schoolbus. Someone handed her a cold can of beer. She croaked a thank you. In Chicago the night before, we had partied late with our friends, screaming above the noise of a disco and she'd awakened with a painful case of laryngitis. I hung back, talking to the reporter, shaking hands, waving at people, milling through the crowd, accepting greetings.

Suddenly a young woman pushed through the mob and made her way to me. Her hair was dark and hung in ringlets around her neck. Her eyes were deep and penetrating. She was about 25 years old and beautiful in an intense, Old Testament way. She stood looking at me, then spoke. "I'm Rachel," she said. Before I could reply, she turned and walked away, disappearing into the crowd. People closed in around me and I was pushed onto the bus. The reporter slid into the seat next to me and I forgot about the young woman outside. Our host found us at last and introduced himself. He was a well-to-do businessman, one of the organizers of the bicentennial celebration.

"Hi kids," he said to our young ones. "My guys are looking forward to meeting you." Then to us: "We'll be dropping you off at our place on the lake. My wife will take good care of you. I'm staying in an apartment in the city." He moved on up the bus to attend to some bicentennial arrangements. Carolyn and I glanced at each other.

"Hmm."

"Hmm, indeed."

I popped open the can of beer someone had pressed into my hand and sat back to enjoy the short ride from the airport. People waved at our garlanded bus as we passed by. Burlington, like the rest of the nation, was in a festive mood.

When we disembarked at the lakeshore, the businessman stayed aboard. Our hostess, a good-looking woman in her late thirties, showed us to our rooms. Lake Champlain was a few steps away from the house. Her kids took our kids in tow and they all got changed into bathing suits and raced toward the water.

Carolyn's throat was getting worse. She went to lie down. I asked our hostess if she knew a doctor we could phone to prescribe some penicillin. "Let me handle it," she said. "You people have the key to the city this week." And sure enough, within ten minutes she had made a call, the doctor in turn had made a call and there was a prescription for antibiotics waiting at the pharmacy in town.

"I'll hop in the Land Rover and go get the medicine," said the businessman's wife. "It won't take me twenty minutes."

"Carolyn is taking a nap. How about if I go along with you?"

She nodded, without much enthusiasm I thought. Something was cooking in her; she seemed distracted, there was unhappiness beneath the pleasant veneer. We pulled out of the driveway and headed toward town. She drove assertively, keeping her eyes on the road and her mouth shut. I sat in the passenger seat next to her with my head against the Land Rover's window, staring at her. Three or four minutes went by as we drove through Burlington's suburbs.

"OK," I said finally. "What's going on?"

She turned and looked at me. "What do you mean?"

"I don't know what I mean. I just figure something's going on that maybe you'd like to talk about."

She looked straight ahead, saying nothing. Then she opened her mouth and babbled for five minutes.

"I can't understand him," she said. "I thought everything was perfect. What does he want? He has an apartment in the city and this house on the lake and a company that's doing great and a wife who loves him and three wonderful kids. What does he want? Maybe it's male menapause." I sat listening to her. She drove smoothly, taking the corners without effort.

"You'd think there would have been at least a hint, wouldn't you? After seventeen years? I mean, I knew he'd been seeing her and that was alright. I have a boyfriend too, for that matter. You'll meet him tonight at the house. There's nothing wrong with that, but you don't have to go breaking up a marriage. And then to move that little chippie in with him. And to take her around to our friends' houses and to all our old restaurants. Is it her youth? What else can he see in a little twit like that? It's beyond me. I don't know. I just don't know."

We drove in silence for a minute or two more, then pulled into the parking lot of a Rexall drug store. She switched off the motor and looked at me, her eyes smoldering.

"Is her name Rachel?" I asked.

A look of total astonishment came over her face. "How in the name of heaven did you know that?"

"I'm psychic," I said. "Come on. Let's get the medicine."

Later that evening, the penicillin and a long nap having done their trick, Carolyn was in fine form again. Our kids and the resident ones, bosom buddies by now, were upstairs watching TV while downstairs, friends of the hostess began to arrive for a welcoming party. We were the happy centers of attraction. Wine flowed, the board groaned and the guests couldn't have been more cordial. The hostess' boyfriend was there (a rustic potter type), along with the doctor who had prescribed for Carolyn and assorted professionals: teachers, artists and the director of the local theater.

Late in the evening, a guy with piercing eyes and a close-cropped beard walked in. He pulled me aside.

"I'm the local Gestalt therapist," he said. (In Burlington?!) "I read your book, *Me and the Orgone*. Very interesting. Here's a copy of the town's underground newspaper. I write articles for it sometimes. You might like to peruse it." He handed me a tabloid and drifted away. Carolyn found me, carrying refills of our wine glasses. I showed her the paper. The headline read: COMMUNAL LESBIANS ASSAIL LESBIAN MONOGAMY. Under that, a smaller headline read: TROTSKYITE SAPPHOS IN ATTACK ON NEO-MIDDLE CLASS LESBIANISM.

Carolyn looked up at me. "Two days of Norman Rockwell Americana?"

On the morning of the 4th, we awoke to the sound of birds singing in the trees outside our window. The parade was to assemble downtown at 9:30 A.M. Our family would ride in a beautiful old convertible with signs taped to its sides: PARADE MARSHALL and ORSON BEAN AND FAMILY. Max clamored to be allowed to sit up front with the driver. Then when the parade began, he turned shy and slumped down in his seat so he could neither see nor be seen.

He reminded me of myself when I was 10. My grandparents had taken me to the circus in Windsor, Vermont, the next town over from Hartland. The magician in the sideshow placed his female assistant in a painted wooden coffin with slots in it, then seemingly pierced her body with 12 to 15 steel swords. The deed completed, he announced that for ten cents anyone in the audience could walk up onto the stage and gaze down into the open box to see how the trick was done. The hayseeds at the sideshow shuffled from foot to foot and stared at the ground, no one wanting to be first.

"Oh please, please," I pleaded with my grandfather. "Let me go up and see how he did it." Grandpa laughed and reached into his pocket to hand me a dime. I raced to the stage, climbed up the four wooden steps to the platform, looked out at the crowd . . . and froze.

"Right this way, son," said the magician in his cape. "The secrets of legerdemain are yours." I stumbled to the box, peered inside for an instant, then walked back down the steps and returned to my grandparents. The ice broken, a line of rubes formed at the base of the steps.

"Well, Dallas, how does the trick work?" asked my grandmother.

"Well . . . well, I . . ." I blushed and stared at my Keds. I had nothing to report. Dying to be first, I had found myself the center of attention (as if anyone cared about the skinny, red-headed city kid in the seersucker shorts) and had become terrified. My eyes had glazed over and I had seen nothing. My grandfather laughed but my grandmother, the more exacting of the two, became annoyed. "Well that certainly was a wasted ten cents," she snapped. "One item less when we get to the refreshment stand, I'd say."

The parade started up, the marshall and his family earning cheers along the way. "Yay, Orson." "Hey, Carolyn, you look beautiful." (She had her own fans from the game show *Tattletales*.) There were cries of "Welcome to Burlington!" and "Happy birthday America!" The procession ended at the town square where a bandstand had been erected on which I delivered a speech on *The Spirit of Ethan Allen*. I worked some of my jokes into the talk, namely a routine about my New England ancestor Ezekiel Bean, who was "the foremost bartender of the American Revolution; Ezekiel Bean *poured* the shot heard 'round the world." The audience loved it. I noticed the Gestalt therapist in the crowd. He was not laughing. I had a wonderful time.

That night there was a Grand and Glorious Pyrotechnical Display at the football field and then, after the kids had been dropped off at home, our hostess and the potter took us out for the evening. The Burlington which I remembered had been transformed. Gone were the Five and Tens and barbershops. In their place stood boutiques and bars and quiche restaurants. We wound up at a country and western joint with live music for dancing. The place was packed but a table was found for the parade marshall. We ordered drinks. The dance floor was crowded. Not far away sat a group of women who drank beer from bottles and occasionally got up to dance with one another. No men came to bother these women.

I pointed out the table to Carolyn. "I wonder if those are the Communal Lesbians?"

"I wonder."

"Well, we'll never know."

"Sure we will. I'll ask one of them to dance." Up she sprang and a moment later she was on the dance floor with one of the better-looking ones.

Our group wound up sitting with their group. They were warm and friendly and bought us beer. They were not the Communal Lesbians.

"Oh no," said one. "I know that bunch of freaks. Weirdos is what they are. We're not like that." She turned to put her arm around the young woman sitting next to her. "I want the same thing as anybody else wants: a house with a picket fence, a color TV and Mary."

For years I had wanted to try LSD. The Sixties had come and gone, but I figured it wasn't too late. I wanted to do the drug with Carolyn, to share the experience with her. Friends of ours from San Diego, a young college professor and his wife whom we liked and trusted, had told us that if and when we were ever ready, they'd get the acid for us, vouch for its purity and stay with us for the twelve hours or so the trip would be likely to take. I said to Carolyn, "We'll never feel more open, trusting and loving than we do right now. If we're ever going to do it, this is the time." She was curious enough about it to agree.

We arranged an all day sitter for the kids and left with our hearts in our throats to meet our friends, the professor and his wife. Their names were Dick and Patsy Peacock. Friends of theirs, who were going to be out of state, had offered to let the experiment take place in their house. It was nine A.M. and the morning sun was already beating down on us as we entered the Peacocks' friends back yard. They lived in the Palisades, not far from our place. The yard was a large space of about half an acre, with a tall fence around it on three sides and the house on the fourth.

Patsy and Dick were waiting for us in the kitchen. He was a man in his mid-thirties, with piercing, intelligent eyes and blond hair. She was a strikingly beautiful brunette in her late twenties. They had recently had twins, she delivering her babies at home, he making a movie of the birth and missing the arrival of the second twin because he'd only expected one child and had had to run out to the drug store for more film. The twins were staying with Dick's ex-wife for the day, while they hosted their friends on an acid trip. Could the whole thing have been more Californian?

Carolyn and I waited nervously for whatever it was to

begin. I was afraid she might change her mind at the last minute, but obviously she had decided to go through with it. Our friend reached into his pocket and pulled out a little package of tinfoil. He unwrapped it and showed us what looked like two tiny specks of wax paper.

"The purest window pane," he said. It meant nothing to me. "Moisten the end of your index finger, pick one up and place it on your tongue." We both did so. I thought I might have dropped mine. I couldn't feel anything dissolving on my tongue.

"It's OK. You've got it."

"What do we do now?"

"Just wait. In about twenty minutes to a half hour, you'll start feeling something." I drank a cup of coffee. Carolyn wandered about the house with Patsy. After a while I walked into the living room and stopped to look at a framed photograph of a sunset over the Pacific. I was surprised to see that the Peacocks' friends had one of those new animated wall photos. As I watched, the sun sank beneath the water and the waves parted to show a giggling, drunken fish.

"Hold everything," I said to myself. I glanced around the room and saw that the furniture was changing shape as if it were being reflected in a Coney Island fun house mirror. I found this hilarious and went looking for Carolyn to tell her what was going on.

"I know," she said. "Look at this tall, skinny lamp." And we both howled with laughter.

I followed Carolyn out the back door and into the sunlit yard. She walked to the center of it, dropped to the ground and lay there face down, her chin propped up in her hands, staring at a little patch of grass. I wandered along the edges of the yard, by the high wooden fence, inspecting the flowering shrubs and bushes, the blossoms of which were incredibly varied and colorful. As I peered at them, the small blooms giggled and tittered, clearly excited by my interest. If I reached out to touch them gently, they thrilled with delight. If I made too sudden a move, they recoiled in fear. They were the most tender, delicate things I'd ever seen.

I looked over at Carolyn who continued to stare at her patch of grass. Twenty minutes went by, or so it seemed to me, and she did not budge from her spot.

"Hey," I called to her.. "Don't stay stuck in that one place all day. There's great stuff going on all over the yard." That half an acre in Pacific Palisades was like Disneyland.

"This is the most fascinating place I've ever seen in my life," she said. "I wish you'd come and share it with me. Either way, I'm staying here." This was a different Carolyn, one that threatened me a bit. She was completely calm and composed. She preferred that I join her but it wasn't all that important. Reluctantly, I walked over and plopped down on the lawn next to her.

"See here." She pointed to an area of about a square inch. "These are the things I'm watching. These two little purple flowers love each other." They were tiny clover-like blossoms, no larger than blades of grass. "The one purple one also has something going on with this yellow flower over here."

"Is the other purple one jealous?"

"No. He knows that what they have together is unique and more important than anything. What she's having with the yellow one is just fun, just a flirtation." I began to stare at the three principals and their supporting cast, an old dandelion who was visibly aging as we watched, and assorted other weeds and grasses.

The area within the square inch that concerned us became more vividly clear to me than anything I'd ever looked at. I could choose to see as much or as little as I wanted. I could focus intimately on the two little flowers and their friends, or I could somehow pull back and view the whole community as if from an observation plane high above.

The two purple cloverlets, in the hours I spent there . . . because I did spend hours there, immobile, lying in the sun, completely immersed and totally content . . . became, to me, the most important things in the living universe. I felt overwhelmed with love and concern for them. Every new little dancing movement, or reaching out to each other, that they performed, thrilled me, filled me with emotion. I cared more for them than I did for Carolyn or for my children or for my own life. Carolyn knew and understood this because she felt the same way. When we would look up from watching the flowers and our eyes would meet, there would be tears of mutually shared happiness in them. There were no feelings of jealousy or possessiveness connected with all of this.

The happiness we felt was a melting one, not jump-up-and-down euphoria, but the kind of peace a holy man in the Himalayas must feel. But what astonished us most was that at exactly the same moment we were experiencing all of this, we knew that sometime in the next day or two, the Japanese gardener would come by with his lawn mower and decimate our little community . . . and we couldn't have cared less.

As we realized that there was really no contradiction in the two attitudes, it seemed to us that we were understanding life, were resolving for ourselves all of the apparent paradoxes which plague the human race. I knew that Carolyn loved me as much as any woman has ever loved a man . . . and that the capacity for total indifference to me was in her. I knew how important I was to my kids *and* that if I got hit by a truck . . . in a few years they might have to dig out a photo to remember what I looked like. I knew how glorious it is to be alive, and how wonderful it will be to die. None of this was intellectual, it was experienced.

Carolyn got up to go into the house to the bathroom. We'd been lying in the yard for hours. I followed her inside. Our friends, the Peacocks, were in the kitchen, waiting in case we needed them. Carolyn came out of the bathroom and accepted the cup of coffee Dick Peacock offered her. For my part, I couldn't bear the separation from my beloved cloverlets a second longer. I headed back out into the back yard and walked toward where they were.

The panic set in slowly, then took me over with a terrible rush. They were nowhere to be seen. I was lost and couldn't find my way home. A wild despair grew in me. I had to find them. I didn't want to face the possibility of life without my little angels, my beloved purple cloverlets. I dropped to my knees and crawled frantically back and forth in the grass. When I realized that finding that square inch in the middle of a half acre of manicured lawn was hopeless and that my darlings were gone forever, a wail of pure grief emerged from my throat.

Carolyn and the Peacocks rushed out into the yard to see what was the matter.

"They're gone, they're lost," I cried, brokenheartedly. Carolyn calmly walked to the exact spot of our little community and sat down next to it. It was six feet from where I was. Overjoyed, I crawled to her, flattening God knows how many other communities in the process. Who cared about them? Who cared if London, Paris and New York were bombed into oblivion? My heart lay in the square inch by Carolyn's right knee.

There they were, oh my God there they were. The dandelion was older now, his stem no longer able to support his fading head erectly. Our two darlings were fine. The yellow friend and lover of the one was OK, too. And the assorted floral characters around them seemed well and happy. The neighborhood was intact. Great tears of relief welled up in my eyes and spilled down my cheeks. I had found them again and must never lose them.

Carolyn went back into the house to finish her coffee. I began studying the terrain. It became the primary goal of my life to be able to find them again at will, not to have to depend on Carolyn to guide me to them. The dandelion was the signpost. Six inches away from it was a dying mushroom. I painfully measured by handspans the distance (seven and a half feet) between the mushroom and a small tree. Convinced that the tree would lead me to the mushroom and it to the dandelion, I ran back to the house, laughing happily. Then I ran back to the tree again, paced off the seven and a half feet and . . . no mushroom.

"Relax, Orson," I told myself. I'd obviously been unclear about the direction from the tree. I searched desperately. The mushroom was gone. Twenty minutes went by and when I realized I wasn't going to find it, a second wail of primordial despair rose from the yard, to send the neighbors to the phone to call the police if the Peacocks couldn't shut me up.

Out they came with Carolyn, and once more she calmly walked to the old spot. This time I studied directions, points of access and visual angles from the house next door. Still, when I started from scratch at the kitchen, I could not make myself find it. Suddenly, the nature of the problem dawned on me: I was trying to *make* myself find the spot, rather than *letting* myself find it. (What an error to make in California.) I went back to the kitchen again, drank some coffee and discussed the situation with the troops. Then I took a few deep breaths, calmly stood up, walked out into the yard and went directly to my little flowers.

I sank to my knees, threw back my head and laughed the way a caveman must have laughed when he rediscovered fire. Never before had I been so exultant and probably never would I be again. And tomorrow, Mr. Osaki would pump a little gas into his mowing machine and murder them all . . . and that was OK too. The Peacocks opened champagne and they and Carolyn came out to help me celebrate.

On the street in front of the house, a Good Humor truck came to a stop, and the tinkling song which called the children to buy ice cream drifted into the yard.

"Oh, look," cried Carolyn, delightedly pointing at our babies. "They're dancing to the music." And sure enough, it was a block party, the old dandelion sitting it out, our two purple sweethearts more in love than ever, swaying rhythmically, the one occasionally turning to include her friend. It was a summer festival, the whole neighborhood celebrating and all in all, one happy square inch of God's green earth.

"They're *getting* the Good Humor," said Carolyn, her face filled with delight and wonder. "I know they are. I can tell. They're actually having ice cream, getting the essence of it somehow. Look how happy they are, like children."

The day moved on, late-afternoon shadows appeared, the old mushroom died; we watched its death, saw it transform, watched its soul move on and exulted in the transformation.

As the shadows grew even deeper, I was alone for a while, staring at a single flower which grew in a spot near the corner of the yard. All at once, a darkness overtook me and I felt a taste of something mysterious and potentially frightening. The face of the flower transformed into a face I knew, had seen before, had always known and always would know . . . and was seeing for the first time. A simian, serpentine, insect-like face it was, not unpleasant, though potentially so . . . in fact, quite beautiful. Unfamiliar, yet terribly known to me, it was. Then I realized that it was a part of my face, a face which every living thing possesses as one of the forms it can and will take.

Suddenly something darker, deeper, perhaps evil began to appear on the face of the flower. I felt myself starting to be drawn in, sucked down into something from which I knew I'd never be strong enough to find my way back. It was dark, terrible and frightening . . . and I realized that it, too, was part of me. I pulled out of the reverie and felt no fear, just a great sense of caution, a realization that anything is possible, but that part of growing is to accept our limitations and not go too far. Black holes are everywhere.

Evening came and we were winding down. We decided the four of us would go to dinner in a restaurant, to complete the trip back into what we call reality. It was eleven P.M. as our friends let us out of their car in front of our house and we started in. I turned on the light outside the door. A little bed of flowers grows there and as I passed by it, I swore a sleepy nasturtium woke up for an instant, smiled at me and then nodded back to sleep.

A few days after our acid trip, there was a story on the front page of the *Los Angeles Times:* MAN SURVIVES 27 STORY PLUNGE IN SAN FRANCISCO. A well-dressed guy, it seemed, had shown up at the Trans-America Building. He was apparently stoned on some drug or other, the paper wasn't sure. He took the elevator up to the 27th floor, to the top of the lobby atrium. He managed to elude the guards and was spotted crawling around on the catwalk, or whatever is up there, I don't remember that part of the story too well. What I do remember is that he missed his footing and fell twenty-seven stories onto the concrete floor of the lobby.

The guards didn't even want to look. They took the elevator down, stopped at the second floor to pick up the dust-pan and broom, and then went to the lobby to clean up the mess. There wasn't any mess. The guy was sitting there with a big smile on his face, singing a little ditty of his own creation called, "Oh What a Trip I'm On." They took him to the hospital and X-rayed him. No internal injuries. At the last minute, the guy had apparently looked down, seen the floor rushing up toward him and, to keep his reality franchise, decided to break his ankles. A few days later, he was released from the hospital and hobbled home. End of story.

Except that two days after that, a man in Vancouver fell twenty-two stories from his hotel room into a swimming pool and didn't even break his ankles. And the day after that, the chute of a G.I. on a training mission failed to open and he fell a quarter of a mile into a haystack and lived to talk about it. These people were dropping like flies. The word was out that falls like that didn't have to kill you. In a week or so, everyone forgot about the story, people went back to dying and the world could relax and breathe easily again.

Truth consists of what *everybody knows.* "You can't fall twenty-seven stories and live." You know it, I know it, The Flying Wallendas know it, *everybody* knows it. But the guy in San Francisco *forgot*. He got stoned and gave himself permission to change the rules. Wow. The other two fallers weren't even *high* (except in altitude).

John Lilly wrote about the altered states of consciousness he'd experienced under acid. Later on, he was able to experience them with no drugs at all, when he blocked out distractions by going into a sensory deprivation tank.

I was home alone one day, sitting in the back yard, thinking about our "trip." Neither Carolyn nor I felt we had hallucinated. We felt the drug had "given us permission" to see some different forms which are always there anyway. Maybe it was crazy. What the hell, "When in California . . ."

It was a sunny afternoon and I was sitting on one of our plastic lounge chairs on the brick patio floor next to the pool. I glanced down at the bricks. Everything has energy in it. Einstein said that and I'd seen it. When I was on acid, even bricks like the ones I was on had seemed to throb. I put down the book I was reading and stared at the bricks. What looked like a slug was crawling across them, changing its direction every few minutes, stopping, then raising up on its hind legs to look around, trying to see where it was headed. It acted more like a caterpillar than a slug. Slugs don't usually seem to care where they're going. Perhaps it was a super slug, on the verge of evolving into something better, like a lung fish crawling out of a pond. Do bugs evolve?

According to the theory of reincarnation, people keep coming back till they've learned all they need to know and have reached perfection. Do bugs come back too? Could a bug learn enough that it would come back as, say, a cat or even a human? Or would it keep reincarnating as a bug until it was the All-Knowing-Bug. Maybe the slug in my yard wouldn't want to evolve into a human. Better to be Super Slug than a coolie in China.

Eastern philosophies teach that even the lowest coolie is perfect. So is a slug. Would I ever understand any of it? I was reading *The Lives of a Cell* by Lewis Thomas. He says we'll probably never be able to understand all there is to know about the digestive tract of the Australian termite.

I looked for my slug but it was gone, having made it across the Mohave patio in some direction or other. When it got to where it was going, had it been content, or had the trip turned out to be a terrible mistake? Had it left family behind? Even a slug must need others of its kind. The effort it had put into traversing such a vast expanse of brick and mortar, perhaps in the wrong direction, reminded me of my own frustrating attempts to improve myself.

I stared at a clump of bushes along the perimeter of the yard and thought about my little purple flowers. We'd driven back to the scene of the crime the next morning. I'd been able to find them in the yard immediately. The gardener had not come by yet. I'd said hello but they hadn't answered. Or, rather, I hadn't heard them. I had no doubt they'd been overjoyed to see me.

I decided to see if I could do what John Lily did and get back in touch with that other reality. I hadn't even had a can of beer. I sat in my patio chair and tried to relax. Then, after a long time, I stopped *trying* to relax and just relaxed. I breathed deeply and fully and told myself to feel at one with the lounge chair, the patio, the sky and the bushes. An hour went by. I thought I detected a rhythmical movement among the leaves of the bushes. Happiness flooded through me. I concentrated on a little bud in the bush nearest to me and it seemed to smile and reach out to me.

I looked down at the patio floor. A slow movement of energy was eddying through the bricks. A much slower, barely perceptible movement was in the mortar between them. I felt connected to it, a part of it. I looked up into the sky. The clouds were glad to see me. Was it only in my mind or was this really happening? Or was the question meaningless?

A beautiful Monarch butterfly passed by. I said hello to it, speaking out loud. I felt that it acknowledged me before it moved on. A moment later, it was back, cruising past, taking me in, out of the corner of its eye.

"Hello, gorgeous," I said, appealing to its vanity. I held out my finger and said to it, "Come on over here so I can get a better look at how beautiful you are." It fluttered on and disappeared around the corner of the house. I waited. Five minutes later it was back, checking me out again, flitting around me, suddenly flying quickly away, high up to the chimney on our roof, then swooping back down in my direction.

Again I invited it to land on my finger. It seemed like a child, interested but shy, or perhaps one whose mother had warned it not to speak to strangers. This flirtation continued for three-quarters of an hour. I was starting to get bored. I stood up. The butterfly was hidden somewhere, no doubt watching me. I said in a loud voice, "All right, butterfly, this is my final offer and I'm not making a penny. Either come onto my finger right now and say a proper hello, or forget the relationship. I'm going inside."

Instantly, the pretty thing appeared from over the top of the house, swooped down and made a perfect landing on my outstretched finger. I was thrilled, I could feel its little legs holding on to me. It opened and closed its wings slowly, seeming to preen itself for my benefit. There was a tear in its left wing.

"Hello," I whispered. Its wings fluttered in response. "OK," I said. "I'm going in now. I'll see you tomorrow." It flew away.

That night at dinner, I recounted my adventures to Carolyn and the children. Susie was not terribly impressed. "Oh, Dad, why do you want to spend the whole afternoon talking to a bug?"

We turned in early. In the morning when I woke up next to Carolyn, the morning sun was shining through a crack in the curtain which covered the window next to our bed.I lay there thinking about my experience of the afternoon before and smiling to myself. It was Carolyn's turn to get up and get the kids off to school, but I decided I'd do it since I was awake anyway. I switched off the clock-radio so it wouldn't wake her when it came on, and continued to lie in bed, luxuriating.

Then I heard, or imagined I heard, the faintest of tap tap taps behind the curtain on the outside of the window. I dismissed it. It happened again. Carefully leaning across Carolyn so as not to disturb her, I drew the window curtain aside. There was my friend, clinging to the window pane and beating on it with his wings. I laughed out loud. Carolyn stirred, grumbling. "I'm sorry, darling," I said, "but it's really worth it. Look who's asking if I can come out and play."

Out I skipped through the bedroom door and he went wild with joy. He instantly landed on my nose, then flew like a shot to the top of the chimney, then dive-bombed me and made three quick passes around my head. Then he flew over and landed on the blue lounge chair where we'd first met. Carolyn, looking on from the bedroom window, shook her head in happy wonderment. I called in to her, "You see? If you work at a relationship, it pays off."

Carolyn got up and cooked bacon and eggs while I spread peanut butter and jelly for the school lunches. We woke the children and I told them what had happened.

"Oh God," said Susie. "You and your insect again. Why can't we have a dog?"

He came every day for two weeks. Carolyn took snapshots of the two of us together, and when I was on *The Tonight Show*, I talked about him and showed one of the pictures. In the weeks that followed, I heard from people all over the country, telling me about butterflies who had befriended them. Others claimed they could talk to animals. One woman wrote to tell me about the cockroaches in her New York apartment. She'd spoken to them and made a deal, she said. She was entertaining that night and didn't want them around. If they'd stay out of sight, she wouldn't spray them. She claimed they'd done what she asked.

My butterfly's wing was getting ragged. He (I couldn't call him it anymore) was flying hard and the strain was showing on the tear. He loved to tease the cat. When she was lying out by the pool, he'd set down not six inches in front of her, and stay very still. Sarah's hopes would be raised. She'd stay equally still except for the involuntary twitching of her tail. A cat's tail is its enemy. Then, as she pounced, the butterfly would hop onto her nose, soar high up to the chimney, then dive-bomb and land on her tail. I'd howl with laughter and the butterfly would make pass after pass around me. Sarah, feigning indifference, would lick herself, all the time keeping an eye on her nemesis.

I sensed he was going away, bid him goodbye one day and told him I'd always remember him. He did, in fact, come back one more time, but then never after that. I felt a real sense of loss. I wondered if he'd gone to that valley in Brazil, where millions of butterflies are supposed to gather. I wondered whether he could make it there with that torn wing of his.

A California year passed and another Monarch came one day. I was sitting out back and he flew right over without being asked, landed on my knee and looked at me, bold as you please. After that, lots of them came to call, dozens and dozens over the next few years, not just to me but to Carolyn, to the kids, to my mother-in-law when she was visiting and to friends who happened to drop by. The word was out in butterfly circles that it was OK.

It never happened except around that house in Pacific Palisades and never with other than the beautiful orange Monarchs. Whenever I've spoken to butterflies anywhere else, they've acted like they were New Yorkers and I was from out of town.

XII

Showing off is an inherently male characteristic, not just with human beings, but throughout the animal kingdom. In virtually all species, the male sports the colors and the plumage. All song birds are males. "Listen to me," they warble. "Ain't I wonderful?" The male lion with his big yellow Afro; the lizard with his bright red pouch; the rooster with his fine feathers and cock's comb; they put on a show like Tom Sawyer walking the fence for Becky Thatcher. They need to convince the females that they're amazing, so they can know it themselves. That's how insecure we males are. We have to put on a whole three-ring circus simply to be able to function.

In the spring, the young male deer sprouts new little horns (he gets horny) and starts checking out the ladies. When his antlers are full grown, he stages fake fights with other bucks to impress the does. Cameras have recorded the fact that the male deer virtually never hurt one another. They are putting on a pageant. Then, when they feel glorious enough, they select a doe and wander off into the woods.

175

Nature provides the male mallard duck with beautiful blue-green feathers so he can impress his (plain brown) female. The peacock is so splendid that his tail is practically in bad taste (I don't want to criticize God). The mandrill monkey is almost pathetic. "How can I convince you that this equipment of mine is wonderful?" he seems to be saying.

The male whooping crane dances for weeks on end to impress his lady and get her to mate with him. (In Baraboo, Wisconsin, at the International Crane Foundation, George Archibald, a keeper to whom a female of that rare and endangered species had formed an attachment, danced for her, imitating male whooping crane movements, for six weeks, 16 hours a day, to get her turned on enough so that she would sit on the egg she'd laid and hatch it. For practical purposes, he became the father of the baby bird that was eventually born.)

In 1981 I was back in New York, alone and feeling sorry for myself, wondering why my marriage had come apart, why Carolyn had had enough of me, pondering the differences between men and women. The New York Marathon was being run; my apartment on Columbus Avenue was a few blocks from the finish line. I wandered over and saw Alberto Salazar beat his own record to become the fastest marathon runner in the world, doing the 26 miles in two hours, eight minutes and thirteen seconds. I watched him stagger across the finish line and collapse, looking more dead than alive, gulping helplessly for air like a beached mackerel, skin pale and sickly looking, hair plastered down, eyes rolling back in his head, saliva dripping from his mouth. It was ten minutes before he was able to speak to the reporters who had gathered around him. His personal need to win had been such that he had driven himself to the outer limits of human endurance.

Seventeen minutes later, Allison Roe crossed the finish line, having done the race in 2:25:28 to become the fastest female marathon runner in the world. She looked radiant.

She spoke to the TV cameras at once, brushing an attrac-
tively wind-swept strand of hair away from her sparkling
eyes and glowing face. She seemed hardly out of breath.

This is the fastest woman in the world, I asked myself?
A hundred and twelve men had managed to cross the
finish line in the time between Mr. Salazar's win and that
of Ms. Roe. Old guys, young kids, skinny runts, short or
tall, they all had one thing in common: they looked like
hell at the end of the race.

Am I saying that men are better than women? Yes.
Better at making damn fools of themselves to prove they
can accomplish whatever they want in this world. There
are fabled cases of mothers somehow finding the strength
to lift pickup trucks off their trapped babies. Women have
the power when the motivation is there, when something
they really want is in it for them. I've always heard that
women should be better at long-distance running than
men are because they have more stamina. But my point is
not that a hundred and twelve guys in that race were fas-
ter than Allison Roe but that they were willing to kill
themselves trying. It wasn't worth it to her to push herself
to the point that she would feel and look truly ghastly in
order possibly to become the fastest person in the world.
She was content to be the fastest *woman* in the world,
and still look swell at the finish line.

I wandered back to my bachelor apartment. There was
no one there to show off for.

Venice, California, 1987

XIII

A friend talked us into laying out a hundred bucks to go to a charity affair at the L.A. Hilton. Oh well . . . it was tax deductible and for a good cause. Eats were first, and then the crowd of six hundred or so moved out to stand on the dance floor and watch the entertainment. Some fairly well-known performers did their thing, and at the end of the show the M.C. announced that there'd be a special surprise.

To introduce it, he brought out onto the stage a large, imposing Black woman who was, it seemed, an evangelist.

"You think you understand life," she thundered at the audience. "You feel proud because you've paid $100 to come here and have a good time and support a worthy cause. You don't understand life! You don't understand charity! You don't understand God!" My eyes met those of a fellow reveler on the dance floor and we smiled uneasily at each other.

The music began to swell. Carolyn and I had been

watching the performance from a spot at the back of the hall. Now we inched closer, moving into the center of the crowd. The evangelist finished her introduction and now directed our attention to stage right. Two young women appeared there, smiling, dressed in blue velveteen frocks. Sisters, they were. Twins. Identical twins. Siamese twins. Joined near the top of the head.

Six hundred people stopped breathing. The girls made their way toward center stage, pressing into each other's foreheads in an upside-down V shape, moving crablike toward the microphone. As they reached it, the pianist hit an introductory chord and they proceeded to sing, in close harmony, two choruses of "You'll Never Walk Alone."

On the dance floor, six hundred people froze between horror and hilarity. Oh God. Oh Jesus. Why us? We paid the money; we came to have a good time. Why did they have to put such a downer on the evening? Christ! To bring those freaks out here. Who's responsible for this? Oh God.

The twins finished their song. The applause hit that middle line between small enough to add to the embarrassment and loud enough to encourage an encore.

But the horror show was not over. Having done their number, the twins now proceeded to step over the footlights, climb down the little flight of stairs at the center of the stage and move out onto the dance floor, directly into the congregation. The crowd parted like the Red Sea. Three hundred people dispersed to the left, three hundred to the right, and the Siamese twins were left alone, still smiling, still moving crablike toward the back of the house.

I clutched at Carolyn's arm. "Look at the bastards run," I said. "Scurrying to get out of the way. Not that I blame them. But as horrible as it was having those freaks inflicted on us, what we're doing to them is worse. I mean, they are human beings."

"Well?" she said.

"All right," I grumbled. "Somebody has to go out there and welcome them. And since nobody else is doing it, I guess it has to be me."

"Good luck."

I walked onto the nearly deserted dance floor. I could feel the eyes of the people on me, staring from the sidelines, and I would rather have been entering the exercise yard at Sing Sing. As I approached the two young women, they looked up.

"Hello, girls," I said. "I'm Orson Bean. You may have seen me on television." (It wasn't easy. I never say things like that, not even to get a good table at a restaurant.)

Recognition and delight spread over their faces. "Oh, wow," they cried. "We watch you on *The Match Game,* and *Tattletales* and *The Tonight Show.*" They were giggling with happiness now.

"I really liked your song," I lied.

"Did you? We worked hard on it. And our mom made these dresses. Yeah, we watch you on TV. We watch TV all the time. In fact, that's what we mostly do. We don't go out a lot." And they both laughed uproariously at this statement.

"Your dresses are very pretty," I said, and realized that I meant it. It occurred to me that I was looking at the girls for the first time now, and as I did so, I was startled to see that they were beautiful. I mean really beautiful. Their eyes were shining with excitement, their smiles were radiant and their happiness seemed quite genuine.

"This is our best night in the world," said one of the them.

"Yeah," said the other. "Fer sure. Fer sure."

California girls, I thought.

We started moving toward the back of the ballroom, and I saw that the strange crab-like gait which had so horrified me on stage was, in fact, an interdependent glide which I now began to think of as graceful and interesting.

They were babbling something about the orchestra, but my mind had flown up and out of the hotel ballroom, high above the sky and far away to another planet where people are joined together in pairs, and where a charity ball is being held and where suddenly—Oh God, oh no. It can't be true. Oh, it's disgusting. Oh look, a freak who's alone. How awful. How could they inflict that on us. How can he live that way? So lonely. So sad. So ugly.

The girls asked me for an autograph. "You should be giving me yours," I said. "You're the stars here tonight."

"Oh wow," they shrieked. "Oh wow!"

Just a couple of California girls, I thought. I bid them goodnight, found my sweet wife and went home.

The Fingers of Fate do their walking through the Yellow Pages of Life in strange and mysterious fashion. If Bob Miller, the young swimming instructor, had failed in the task the YMCA had assigned him, he had succeeded gloriously in one of which it would scarcely have approved. Each afternoon, when his abortive lessons were finished and Zeke, released from his torment, had dashed into the house, Carolyn would emerge from the kitchen with a tray of tuna sandwiches on paper plates, garnished with cold cans of Olympia beer.

I was, by this time, writing a regular column for the *L.A. Free Press,* a muckraking counterculture newspaper. I did this every day in a window-filled cupola over our living room. The only room on the second floor of our house, it had been added by the previous owner, an architect, as an office for himself. It was reached by an outside stairway near the pool.

"Orson, do you want to join us?" Carolyn would call. I never did. Stopping for lunch was anathema to me. It took me long enough to start writing every day. I was happy to look out the window and see my beautiful wife playing gracious hostess to the frustrated young swimming instructor.

One day, two weeks into the futile instructions, I took a break from my work just as Carolyn and Bob Miller were finishing their lunch. I passed them on my way to the kitchen, where I was headed to replenish my upstairs supply of instant coffee.

"Hi Orson," said Bob as I went by. "How's the writing

going?"

"Hard . . . but they're paying me $35 a column so I've got to hang in there."

I continued into the kitchen, then glanced out the window and saw my wife and the young man in the Speedo bathing suit gazing into each other's eyes. It suddenly dawned on me that the electrical charge between them could have illuminated all of L.A. and parts of Orange County.

Old-fashioned jealousy sank its fangs into my belly. As I watched, Bob stepped into our outside shower, then came out a moment later wearing his patched blue jeans and a "Palisades Y" T-shirt. Picking up his motorcycle helmet from a plastic lounge chair by the pool, he headed into the house. Carolyn walked next to him. They passed through the living room and then on out the front door to the driveway, where his motorcycle was parked. I felt my eyes shrink to the size of a pair of BB's. With studied casualness, I strolled into the living room. From there, I could look out the front window and see Bob starting up his motorcycle in the driveway. Carolyn was standing two or three feet from him, smiling entrancingly. There was no physical contact between them; there didn't have to be.

As the Honda 750 roared away, Carolyn re-entered the house. She passed me on her way to the kitchen, humming a little tune to herself, oblivious, of course, to the feelings that were coursing through me. What was I to do? This was what I had theorized about endlessly in Australia. Should I lay my fifty cents on the counter, or shut up and pretend I'd noticed nothing? I didn't like the way I felt: mean, grasping and possessive. It made my forehead ache and my stomach feel tight. So what if they were turned on to each other? Did that really take anything from me? Carolyn and I had, in fact, I now remembered, been making passionate love almost every night for the past two weeks. I suddenly realized that I owed part of my good fortune to her new friend, the swimming instructor. A resentful knot tied itself in my solar plexus. I felt a sense of betrayal.

Wait a minute, I reasoned. Wasn't I getting the benefit of Carolyn and Bob's attraction to each other? If I could let go of the *idea* that it was a bad thing for my wife to desire someone else, the *fact* of it seemed to be good for everyone involved. *Unless she wanted him instead of me.* That thought pulled the knot inside me even tighter. But she *didn't* want him instead of me. She had been really turned on to me lately. She apparently wanted him in addition to me.

The knot in my solar plexus began to loosen up. Suddenly I felt excited . . . actually sexually excited. Was I some kind of a weirdo? Well, I obviously couldn't be *indifferent* to Carolyn's attraction to Bob. So that left me with two choices: I could go on feeling angry and jealous or I could let myself be happy and excited.

I followed Carolyn into the kitchen and sat down at the table in the corner. She was scraping carrots into the trash bin. I waited a bit, then spoke.

"You two are pretty attracted to each other, aren't you?"

She looked up from her carrots. "Why do you say that?"

"Because it's true. It's obvious from the way you look at each other."

"Well, I guess we are a bit turned on, but we certainly aren't going to do anything about it."

"Why not?"

"For one thing, I'm almost ten years older than he is. What makes you think he'd want to, even if I did?"

"Don't play dumb. You know he's attracted to you."

"He's never said so."

"Of course he hasn't. Not in so many words. He's being decent. You're a married woman and he respects me . . . all that stuff. But it's obvious."

Carolyn walked to the table and sat down across from me.

"Well," she said, "the main reason I'm not going to do anything about it is that you and I are really feeling good together and I don't want to spoil that."

"But this is exactly what we went through all that madness about back in Australia."

"How would you feel if I did want to?"

"I'd feel a little anxious, I guess . . . and I'd be able to handle it."

"Are you sure?"

"Honey, I'm not sure of anything. The point is, I'd be willing to try."

Carolyn didn't answer, and since I had nothing more to say for the moment, we let the matter drop.

The next afternoon, Bob showed up at the usual time. From my nest on the second floor, I watched him tool into the driveway on his bike. I yelled a quick hello. Zeke was already out at the pool. Carolyn stayed in the kitchen, not coming out to meet him, as was her usual custom. "Hmm," I mused. "The plot does not grow thinner." I made a decision. My latest column was finished. Slipping it into a manila envelope, I went downstairs and found my wife.

"I'm going in town to drop this copy off at the *Free Press* and do a few other things. I'll be back in three hours."

Her eyes looked searchingly into mine. "I love you, sweet woman," I said. "Have fun." I gave her a hug, walked out the door, climbed into the van and sped off in the direction of Hollywood. Two blocks away, a member of the L.A.P.D. pulled me over and gave me a ticket for going 42 in a 30-mile zone.

"Really," I thought. "What's my hurry?"

I spent a great deal of the rest of the afternoon trying to remember the name of an insect I'd read about, which is born, matures, mates, grows old and dies . . . all in the space of three hours. I thought about how Albert Einstein had shown that under certain circumstances time appears to slow down. I didn't imagine that Einstein had ever sent his wife off to fool around with the swimming instructor. What the hell am I doing, I asked myself? My heart was pounding. I felt continuous excitement, interspersed with flashes of terror. I didn't know what to expect when I got home, or what I really wanted.

I drove to Hollywood, dropped off my column, flirted with the *Free Press* receptionist for a while and then went to a Sunset Boulevard lunch counter, where I ordered a grilled cheese sandwich and a vanilla milk shake. In moments of stress, my body craved those foods which had soothed it in my childhood.

When I finally got home, I found Michele, Susie and Zeke watching television in the playroom. Max was down the street at a friend's house, they told me. And there was a note for me from Mom in the bedroom. She'd gone off somewhere with the swimming teacher. I swallowed hard, made my way to the bedroom and found the envelope on my dresser. I opened it. "Darling," it read. "I love you more than anything in the world. Please know that. I want to stay with you forever. You are my Prime Rib. I've gone to have a bit of popcorn. Home by five. Yours always. Carolyn."

At twenty minutes of six, Bob Miller's motorcycle roared into our driveway. Carolyn's arms were wrapped tightly around his waist. She looked radiant. I didn't know whether to laugh or cry. She jumped off the motorcycle before it had come to a complete stop and rushed into my arms.

"Oh, I love you, Orson. I love you so," she whispered.

"Did you have fun?"

"Yes, and I can't wait to get you alone."

Bob had by then propped his Honda up on its kickstand. He approached me, removing his helmet, offering his hand. His eyes were sparkling, his grin looked sheepish.

"This is some lady you've got here, Orson. You're a lucky man, my friend."

"I know." I shook his hand.

"I hope you do, man. She's really crazy about you."

"Bob! Bob!" Zeke and Susie had come running out of the house. "Give us a ride on your motorcycle." The swimming instructor looked at Carolyn.

"Alright. Once each around the block." She pulled my hand, dragging me into the house.

"Do you really love me?" I asked. "Honestly?"

"Oh, God, I do. I do. If I had to choose, it would be you a million times over. In fact, I know now more than ever how much I love you."

"Was it better with him than it is with me?" I knew it was a stupid question, but couldn't keep from asking it.

"Oh, darling. Say you'll be my main course always. And right now, I'm starving for roast beef . . . *au jus*, if you please."

"Send your friend home, will you? I need to have you all to myself right now."

"I will, dearest. I will."

I walked back into the house. My heart was pounding in my shirt. We're explorers on a new frontier, I thought. A new Lewis and Clarke. I went into the bedroom and waited for my wife. We had entered a new phase of our life together.

I was beginning to realize "what's wrong with this picture." I was wife swapping with an unmarried man. Bob Miller didn't even have a girlfriend. Correction. He had. It was my wife. The casual turn-on had blossomed into a full-fledged romance. When there weren't daytime or evening trysts, there were phone calls and love letters. There were afternoon walks on the beach and trips on the motorcycle to watch him play basketball with his friends.

And the thing is, he was adorable. He was a perfect gentleman. When I wasn't busy hating him, I loved him. And though it may seem odd, the sex was the easiest part of it to deal with. Carolyn was in love with life and voracious to be made love to, and I was getting the major benefit of all this sexual/emotional turn-on. As long as I looked at it rationally, I knew that I was wonderfully well off. It was Carolyn who had the hard job: juggling two lovers, the old buck and the new young stud; keeping both of us happy, satisfied and reassured.

What a reasonable and splendid fellow I was. But one afternoon I wandered into her sewing room to see if she had found time to patch my torn old blue jeans, and discovered that *his* jeans had somehow wormed their way into the clothing pile . . . and been attended to first. I thought I would go berserk. I hardly spoke to her for the rest of the day. It required her preparation of roast lamb and mashed potatoes (my real-food equivalent of grilled cheese sandwiches) even to begin to calm me down. And, of course, the instant rehabilitation of my torn Levis.

I entered into a subtle competition with Carolyn's lover. He had a pierced ear; I got Carolyn to pierce mine. She was an expert at it . . . had pierced her own and those of her daughters. She gave me one of her diamond studs. I then carried my self-adornment a step further and got a tattoo. It happened when I was appearing on a talk show with a widely known tattoo artist from San Francisco. His name was Lyle Tuttle and he had planned to demonstrate his artistry on a volunteer. At the last minute, the volunteer had chickened out.

"You can put one on me," I told him, live on the air. I made an on-the-spot decision to wear a small yellow rosebud on my forearm forever. "Your permanent prom corsage," Carolyn called it. She always managed to keep a sense of humor about my excesses. I tried to talk her into getting a matching tattoo: "A little yellow rosebud of your own, right there on your chest." She declined: "I'd hate the thought of watching it slowly turn into a long-stemmed rose."

I made the mistake, one night, of going out for beers with a male friend to discuss the amorous complexities of my marriage. He listened, then summed up his view of my life succinctly. "You're a schmuck," he said.

I decided I had to have sex with another woman. The fact that I really didn't want sex with another woman, that it was all I could do to keep up with Carolyn, that I had put myself in competition with a man 23 years younger than myself . . . all these things became irrelevant. What counted was that the situation "wasn't [as my children loved to say] fair."

I didn't have the remotest clue how to go about finding a woman. I hadn't seriously approached one in over ten years. I had heard of a place in the mountains of Topanga, called Sandstone. It was an Esalen with sex. Our old friend Gay Talese had lived up there for a few months, doing research on his endlessly awaited tome on the sexual revolution in America. Alex Comfort and Max Lerner had written about it. I told Carolyn I wanted us to go there. She curled her lip and rolled her eyes, but agreed to go. It was, after all, "only fair."

I looked up the number, called, told the man on the phone who we were, and that Gay Talese was a friend of ours. People normally required a pre-interview, he said, but they would make an exception in our case: we could come to the "party" on Saturday night. I suppose he figured that celebrities were a safe bet, did not carry communicable diseases. I don't know what an in-person interview could have told him anyway, other than that we didn't weigh 300 pounds apiece or have some gross affliction like Dr. Johnson's missing syphilitic nose.

We should be prepared to pay a $25 guest fee, he said, bring a salad or casserole for the potluck dinner, wine if we wished . . . no hard liquor or drugs . . . and a towel for swimming.

"And a bathing suit?" I asked. There was a barely perceptible pause, then . . .

"If you like," said the man. "Anything goes at Sandstone."

When Saturday arrived, we were gripped by terror. Carolyn had prepared her famous tuna curry casserole. I had invested in a flagon of Sebastiani chablis. We had packed a canvas bag with two enormous, fluffy towels . . . and no bathing suits.

The sun was about to set as our van turned off the Pacific Coast Highway and began the long, tortuous climb up into the Topanga Mountains. As we left civilization behind, the views became astonishing. The early evening sky gradually darkened. We arrived at a turn in the dirt road where what we saw literally took our breath away. In the foreground were mountains out of pre-history. Great monolithic shards of rock jutted up, leaning against one another as if for support. No vegetation grew on these, no light flickered on them; it was as if life had not yet appeared on the planet. Behind them, in 180-degree panoramic display, was the vast, neon-lit city of Los Angeles. The contrast was beyond art or nature.

Up we drove, following the instructions we'd been given on the phone, climbing the mountain. A pony-tailed hippy waved at us in the fading light. We passed horse pastures and a geodesic dome. Finally, we turned into a private drive between two great stone posts, made our way down a deeply rutted driveway and came to a parking lot with perhaps 30 cars in it. Above it, up a steep incline, was a large ranch-style building, flanked by several smaller ones . . . and of all things, a wigwam. Standing in front of the wigwam was a furry, beautifully tanned, handsome young man, completely naked except for a feather in his hair. He bounded toward us, smiling and extending his arms.

"Hello, beautiful people from down the hill," he said. "My name is Conan. I live here." He embraced Carolyn with a warm and loving hug. Then he embraced me with a warm and loving hug. I tried to remember if I had ever been hugged by a naked man before. Offhand, I couldn't recall its having happened.

"What do you call yourselves?" he asked.

"I'm Carolyn."

"I'm Orson."

"Come with me, Carolyn and Orson, and I'll introduce you to the other loving people here at Sandstone." He took Carolyn's casserole from her. We began the steep climb to the main building, following Conan up a flagstone path.

"Do a lot of people live here?" I asked.

"There are 15 of us right now. Five couples, two singles and a threesome. I'm single." He smiled invitingly at Carolyn. "The residential community is one-third of what goes on here at Sandstone. We're an experiment in New Age living, and we also keep the grounds up. The next third is seminars. Where people learn to be more open. These are led by our director, Paul Paige. He's a Gestalt therapist and a great man. He allows no one to smoke dope up here . . . but he never comes into my teepee." Again he smiled at Carolyn. "The third part of Sandstone is the Wednesday and Saturday night parties. That's what you beautiful people are here for. These parties are attended by the outside members of Sandstone: mostly professional people. What do you do?" He was looking at me.

"I'm an actor on television."

"Oh that's wonderful. I'll have to run electricity into my teepee and borrow a TV set."

"So what happens at these Wednesday and Saturday night parties?" I asked, trying to sound casual.

"Whatever you like, so long as you act lovingly and respect one another's space."

"What about sex?" I didn't know if I sounded more like a hayseed or a dirty old man.

"If you want," said Conan. He smiled at Carolyn again. "I'd like to have sex with you, if you like. You are very beautiful. Would that be alright?"

"Well, uh . . ." said Carolyn, "Uh, let's see how it all goes. This is our first time." She sneaked a glare at me.

"Alright," said Conan. We climbed in silence for a moment, then he continued. "The parties here at Sandstone are different from any other parties. At a regular party down the hill . . . a cocktail party in Malibu, say . . . if you ran around trying to make love to everyone, you'd be a social disgrace. At a swingers' party in the valley, if you *didn't* run around trying to make love to everyone, you'd be a social disgrace. At Sandstone, either is alright. Or anything else. As long as you respect one another's space. We have members who come here just to listen to the music or watch the sunset. And that's alright, too."

We had arrived at a porch, which led to a door through

which we now came into a very large room containing fifteen or twenty people in various stages of undress. An attractive, naked young man approached us, smiling warmly, extending both hands to offer us a hug of welcome. He was followed by a slim, beautiful and equally naked young woman.

"I'm Marty," said the man, "and this is my wife, Sue." Now Sue pressed her tanned-all-over body against Carolyn's and then against mine, enveloping us in her embrace. I glanced at Carolyn. She seemed to be taking it all in stride. I wondered if my face showed the stupefaction I felt.

"Put your food over there," said Marty, indicating a long buffet table to our right. "There are lockers downstairs where you can stash your bag. Then come back up and we'll get our little bit of paperwork out of the way. After that, I'll introduce you to some of our members." Conan smiled goodbye and placed Carolyn's casserole on the table alongside a collection of other dishes. As he did so, he directed our attention to a stairway which led down to the lockers.

On the wall facing us was a huge stone fireplace in which a cheery fire blazed, more for effect than warmth apparently, since the evening was balmy. On either side of the fireplace were the ubiquitious California sliding glass doors. These led onto what looked like a large wooden deck. We could see a couple sitting on the rail of this deck.

Following Conan's directions, we headed downstairs, happy to be off by ourselves for a moment. As we descended the staircase, we passed a hand-lettered sign, which read QUIET DOWNSTAIRS PLEASE. LOVE ONLY BEYOND THIS POINT.

"What do you think so far?" I asked Carolyn.

"Pretty weird."

"But they all seem friendly."

"Too friendly."

At the bottom of the stairs, we found ourselves in a long, dark room, illuminated only by dim red lights. On the floor of both sides of the room were mattresses, lined up one alongside another. On the mattress nearest us were three people: two men and a woman. The woman lay with her head on the lap of one man, and was caressing the face of the other man. None of them had any clothes on. They paid no attention to us. We turned to our right and entered a small locker room.

"Hmm," I said to Carolyn.

"Hmm," she said to me. We left the canvas bag of towels in an open locker, closed it . . . there didn't seem to be any locks . . . then walked past the three lovers and back up the stairs. I carried the jug of Sebastiani chablis in my hand, a totem to ward off undue excitement.

Marty was waiting at the top of the stairs. He escorted us to a little desk near the door we'd entered and gave each of us a form to fill out . . . address, date of birth, etc. Then he took our $25.

"Let me show you around," he said. "This is the main room, where we'll eat our dinner and where we dance or just hang out. And this is the deck." He walked us through the open glass door. The moon had risen, even though it was not quite dark yet. It was an almost full moon and the view was spectacular, as had been all the views we'd seen that evening: mountains beyond mountains and in the distance, the Pacific.

"Down here . . ."—he pointed over the rail—"is our king-sized Jacuzzi. It can hold twenty people."

"We crammed thirty-four in there one night," piped up a woman who'd been standing near us. Marty laughed.

"This is Helen and . . ." indicating a bearded young man behind her, "that's Jim. These are the Beans, Carolyn and Orson." The four of us exchanged greetings.

"On up the hill, a bit," Marty continued, "there's another building which houses our olympic-sized pool. The smaller building next to it is where we have our educational seminars . . . there and in the pool or in the Jacuzzi. Downstairs is the romantic, quiet area. The room you saw on your way to the locker area has mattresses, along the walls. If you're on one of these mattresses, the implication is that you are not open to being joined. Of course, you may always invite some-one . . . or more than one . . . to join you.

"There's a room beyond that, which you may not have seen. It's completely filled with mattresses. If you're in there, the implication is that you *are* open to being joined. Of course, you're always free to say no. The rule here is 'respect one another's space.' Aside from that, not much is spelled out.

"Once in a great while someone, usually female, starts to feel ganged up on or pressured. When that happens, there's always someone else nearby to step in and inter-vene. But that's very rare. It all takes a bit of getting used to. You may learn a lot about yourselves up the hill here at Sandstone."

Marty conducted us back into the main room. He intro-duced us to a good-looking middle-aged couple: "This is Len and Myra. They are about the nicest people you'll get to know up here. And they can tell you anything I've left out."

Len recognized me from *The Tonight Show*. Myra knew both of us from the afternoon *Tattletales* program. They were sweet, supportive, full of information, and after a while we began to relax with them. It was dinner time then. We all lined up at the buffet table with paper plates. There was lots of good food. Myra raved about Carolyn's tuna curry just like any nice lady might, and in time I was able to stop stealing glances at her beautiful naked breasts.

We were introduced, as the evening progressed, to most of the people in the room. Some of them had their clothes on, as did we. Others were nude. Most had at least some-thing on. One naked man spent the whole night parading back and forth with a perpetual erection which had a full-sized bath towel draped over it. No one paid any attention to him.

When the meal was finished, somebody turned on disco music and the dancing began.

"Why don't we sneak down and take a Jacuzzi while

everyone's busy up here," I whispered to Carolyn.

"Good idea. Let's do it." We quietly got up and stole downstairs. No one was lying on the mattresses. We undressed, stuck our clothes in the locker, wrapped the big towels around ourselves and slipped out through the door. There was a chill in the air now. We were high up the mountain and the sky was very clear. Hundreds of stars twinkled and the nearly full moon shone brightly. We slipped off the towels and stepped into the hot water.

"You're the best-looking woman in the joint," I whispered. She laughed, pleased. We turned on the bubbles, then sat enjoying the warm water, cool air and glorious sky.

After a while I said: "Want to go back upstairs and have a dance?"

"Not really. I don't feel like getting dried and dressed up again."

"We don't have to get dressed up again. We could go up there like this."

"You mean naked?"

"Well, we could wear our towels."

"We can't dance in towels."

"We can try. And if they fall off, so what? We're here to have the experience of Sandstone. And right now, this seems to be what it is."

To make a long story if not short, gentle reader, at least less than interminable, we did go upstairs. We danced. Carolyn tried to keep the towel around her but it kept falling off. We laughed. We threw the towels away and danced naked. Other people asked us to dance. Naked people. At first it was embarrassing; then it was liberating. Finally, it was just plain fun.

Late in the evening, we wound up back downstairs. My wildest fantasies were about to come true, when like a schmuck I started giggling. I glanced over at Carolyn. She started giggling too. I nodded my head in the direction of the door. Carolyn nodded back. We contained our laughter until we were safe in the locker room. Then we howled, muffling the sound as best we could with our towels.

"Let's get dressed and get the hell out of here," I said. "I want you back in our bed and I want to make love to you."

"That sounds good to me," said Carolyn.

We drove carefully back down the hill.

XIV

It is the time of the Spanish Inquisition and a man is locked in a dungeon. He has been there for years and is going to stay there until he dies. The dungeon is three stories below ground. The moss-covered walls are damp and clammy, his only company the rats and scorpions that share his cell. Once a day, a silent jailer unlocks his door and leaves him a tin plate with something filthy to eat on it. If he tries to speak to the jailer, he is struck. The prisoner has forgotten how many years he has been there. He has forgotten his anguish at the realization that he would never again see the sun or hear a bird sing or smell a flower or touch a woman or listen to the sound of a human voice.

Lately, the jailer has been drunk. Sometimes he strikes the prisoner with no provocation. Occasionally, he forgets to bring his food. One day, he throws the plate of food onto the slick floor of the cell, slams the door shut and neglects to lock it. The prisoner's heart stops. He remains motionless, afraid to hope. After a while, he hears the sound of snoring. He pushes on the cell door. It moves slightly, making a grating noise. He freezes in terror, his mind racing wildly. The jailer continues to snore. The prisoner opens the door wide enough to slip through. Halfway down a long, dark hall, lit by a flickering torch stuck into the wall, the jailer is asleep in a chair. The ring of keys dangles from his belt. The prisoner is afraid his heart will burst with excitement. He slowly creeps toward the sleeping jailer, sure that the beating of his heart will awaken him.

The prisoner reaches for the keys. The jailer stirs. He freezes, then, when the snores resume, he hooks a finger through the key ring and lifts it from the jailer's belt. At the end of the hall is an iron door. The third key he tries fits and he finds himself at the bottom of steep, winding, stone steps. He is afraid he will collapse with excitement. Is it day or night outside? Will he see the sun or the stars? He has no idea. He races up the steps and comes to another iron door. He chooses a key, it works, he pushes open the door and is free.

They are waiting for him outside the door. Two guards seize his arms. A Bishop of the Church steps from behind them.

As the prisoner is led back to his dungeon cell, he hears the sound of a human voice for the first and last time when the Bishop speaks to him.

"Without hope, my son, there can be no true despair."

Venice, California, 1987

XV

In my fancy days back in New York, I was a Marlboro man. To light my cigarettes I employed a gold Cartier lighter. Simple, slender and elegant, it was my pride and joy. At cocktail parties, I'd whip it out and ostentatiously light up. "Ooo," someone next to me would always say. "That lighter is a beauty. May I see it?" With hawk eyes, I'd watch my prize as the stranger examined it.

"Can I have a light please?" Now someone else was fondling the beautiful lighter. When it was finally safe, back in my pocket, I'd sigh with relief. Then I'd check on it all evening, patting the side of my pants to feel its reassuring shape. The thing was driving me nuts. Thank God, someone finally stole it. Of course I was grief stricken.

What did I buy next? A 69¢ Bic. Nice, plastic, bright red, made in the U.S.A., thousands of lights from a single Bic. And when I lost it, pfft. Who cared?

So, what was the lesson I learned from my two lighters? That it was better to have the Bic than the lighter from Cartier? Don't be ridiculous. It was better to have the gold lighter, but with a Flick Your Bic *attitude*. Then, instead of going around grumbling, as I had done: "For three years I had a Cartier lighter but someone ripped it off," I could have told people, "I had a wonderful cigarette lighter once, for *three years*." Wow.

OK, folks. Listen. I had a wonderful wife once, for fourteen years.

It is said that in a seven-year period the human body completely rejuvenates itself. At the end of that time, every cell has been replaced by another just like it and we have become, in a way, a whole new person. For the first seven years Carolyn and I were together, we saw each other infrequently: I was a workaholic, she the dutiful, stay-at-home wife. Our second seven years were entirely different: we became inseparable.

Both of us had always feared desertion. We had each been rejected by the parent of the opposite sex. What I learned as a little kid was that women are dangerous, so you'd better keep an eye on them. What Carolyn learned was that men tend to leave, so if you want them to hang around you'd better be perfect. Pressure slowly built up as it had on Krakatoa West of Java. Finally the marriage exploded, showering the family with debris.

Nothing worked any more. The passion drained out of our love life. We no longer slept like spoons. I couldn't believe what was happening. It had never occurred to me that we wouldn't always be together. Whatever problems arose could be solved: I would figure out what needed to be done, explain it to Carolyn and she would do it. She didn't want to listen. She was through. I moved out of our beautiful house and into a little place we owned in Venice. We ran to a marriage counselor. It didn't help.

I drowned in grief. Such was my miserable state of mind that when my theater agent called with a job in Knoxville, Tennessee, I accepted. What difference did it make? I stayed there for eight weeks, rehearsing and performing an earthbound comedy and deciding that if a doctor ever gave me a short time to live, I would return to Knoxville so it would seem longer.

Back to Venice then, to my little nest in the canals. The children were wonderful, caring and supportive of both of us. A torrent of guilt welled up in me. Should I try to hold the family together at all costs? I began to have dreams of my mother's sticking her head in the oven while I refused to turn off the gas. I agonized over what had caused the breakup. A friend, Herb Goldberg, who writes best sellers about men and women, tried to help me understand.

Beneath the Beans' offbeat, eccentric behavior, he explained, we had, in fact, enjoyed the most traditional of marriages. I was Head of the Family, decision-maker, provider, protector, Carolyn the passive, smiling helpmate. When we broke up, we did so not for the obvious reasons: the open relationship, constant change, lack of financial security. Our marriage fell apart, said Herb, for the same reason that more than half of all American marriages are collapsing these days: sexual role playing.

Women, taught to be afraid of their own aggressiveness, are drawn to men who seem to be strong, fearless and independent. Men, taught never to admit need, choose women with a mothering quality and the seeming ability to figure out what a man wants without his even having to ask for it. This destructive "gender conditioning," as Herbie calls it, creates a polarization: the man becomes the actor, the woman the reactor. It begins on the first date.

I pursued Carolyn and asked her out. I picked the restaurant, chose the food and wine from the menu, paid the bill, then made my move and seduced her. At least, that's what I thought I did. She was the one who put on the low-cut dress and the perfume. We started that night on a fifteen-year-long game of mutual manipulation. Well, what else could we do? It was all we'd ever been taught.

Thinking back, I realize I never once asked myself whether our interests matched or our choice of friends was compatible. (A running gag of ours in the early days was: "What we have in common is that neither of us likes to ski.") Instead, I paid attention to the fact that she was gorgeous and would look great on my arm, that she would make a good mother to the large family I'd always wanted (I checked out how she related to Michele and was pleased on that score), that she didn't have much dough and would therefore be snowed by the fact that I had a lot, and most important, that she would apparently (without its being acknowledged) be dependent enough on me to put my needs over hers.

I imagine Carolyn had a comparable check-list of her own: I was attractive, I had money and the potential to earn more, I was a celebrity and moved in exciting circles, I would make a good father to her children (I was clearly devoted to my own daughter) and I was obviously dependable. A good catch. I turned Carolyn into a sex object (which bolstered my "masculinity"). She turned me into a success object (which compensated for her fear of independence, aggression and power). It's what we had been programmed to do from the beginning.

We were good and loving people: honest, hard working and sincere. We gave the marriage our all, raised wonderful children and had fabulous adventures. But the seeds of destruction were built in to the very essence of how we related. The qualities she originally found attractive in me: my strength and dependability, the feeling that I would "take over and make everything alright," she came in time to hate, feeling herself controlled, with her identity annihilated. I, in turn, came to resent her dependence on me, to feel oppressed by the unending responsibility, exhausted from always having to be in charge.

I was devastated by the breakup, crawled into a hole to lick my wounds. Carolyn went out and partied. She experienced her new-found anger as a great relief. Mine was suppressed, clouded with guilt, the guilt all men suffer when they go through divorce. They have been the dominant ones, have made the decision (they believe), have taken responsibility for the little woman and the kids. Now they must shoulder the blame when things don't work out. At least, that's what Herb Goldberg says.

So, is Herb, the expert, correct? Oh Herbie, I dunno. It all sounds right but the fact is I honestly don't understand what happened to us and why we came a-cropper. (Certainly it wasn't Carolyn's affair with Bob Miller. That ran its course and he remains a good friend to both of us.) Love is a mystery. No expert knows what makes a man and woman spark together; nor can he say why the magic goes away. We had burned the candle of our marriage at both ends, crammed lifetimes of passion and adventure into fourteen years. Friends have asked me why our marriage failed. Was *My Fair Lady* a failure? We ran twice as long. I think it was the greatest marriage in history. What does Carolyn think? Something else, no doubt. Men and women are different. Carolyn and I are different. Our experiences were not the same; she would write another account of our life together.

I don't regret anything, including the mistakes and the excesses. I don't regret the pain we put each other through, which I have chosen not to deal with in this book. I forgive us for everything. I forgive God and Senator Joe McCarthy and Vlad the Impaler, too. But most of all, I forgive myself. That's a big lesson to learn in this world, and I'd never have learned it if I hadn't had to go on living without my Carolyn.

We did the obligatory legal stuff. (Old Mexican curse: May your life be filled with lawyers.) We made our settlement and divided our property, sharing legal custody of the children. In the words of Caitlin Thomas, I had "left-over life to kill." A call from my agent sent me flying to New York to do a television "voice over." As if I weren't depressed enough, he had booked me a room at the Roosevelt Hotel. Every other hotel in town was filled with conventioneers. I could have bunked in with friends but couldn't bear to face them. I walked alone through the city in which I had spent twenty glorious years, hating it, feeling like a stranger.

I was on my way to my agent's office on 57th Street. I stopped to look in the window of a store, not because there was anything that interested me there, but because with every step I took, it seemed as if my broken heart would just refuse to go on pumping blood through my body. I saw my reflection in the window of the store and, to my absolute astonishment, I looked beautiful. I rubbed my eyes and looked again. For the second time in my life, as it had that day seventeen years before in Ireland, a feeling of total peace of mind and well-being flooded through me. I knew . . . *knew* . . . that everything was going to be fine, no matter what happened. Once again I was totally immersed in where I was at that precise moment in time. Suddenly, New York was The Emerald City of Oz. What an adventure to be there. What a joy to be alive. I left the store window and walked on. I was glad to be going to see my agent. Everyone in the street looked beautiful. I said hello to people as I passed them and they answered me. I glanced at my reflection in each store window I passed, marvelling at the wonder of myself.

This time, the happiness lasted for about an hour and then slowly faded, but now I knew that what I'd experienced was not a miraculous, one-shot occurrence, but that it should be theoretically possible to feel like this all the time. I "knew" that joy was the natural state of things and that misery and resignation are unnecessary.

I decided to move back to New York and return to my first love, the theatre. Max spent the first six months there with me, to help me through them, bless his heart. Then he flew back west to be with his beloved mom and the other kids. Michele, a beautiful young woman now, went to Paris to spend some time with her mother.

I looked for work on Broadway. It was harder to come back than I'd expected. Well, what the hell. As my grandfather used to say: "If it was easy, *everybody* would do it. *Hard* is what keeps out the riff-raff." I stopped all appearances on TV, wanting to concentrate exclusively on theatre. Whenever I could, I flew to the coast to see the kids, or had them come back east. Things were rough between me and Carolyn. We both wanted them not to be. It took time. Little by little, they got better.

When I'd first gone to California, I had done EST (of course), where they teach you that while you can't always have what you want, you can always learn to want what you have. Now I began to be able to put this into practice. I started, to my amazement, to feel happy sometimes for *no reason*. But the feeling would slip away when I fell into a funk about Carolyn. I remembered the story of the prisoner, from a long-forgotten book I'd read as a boy. "Without hope, there can be no true despair." Why could I not let go, accept my life as it was, and allow myself to be consistently happy? More and more, it seemed to me that simply to be happy was all there was to learn in this life. Someone once wrote that three straight days of continuous joy may be the most revolutionary act possible.

I thought about all the values and beliefs I had chewed up and swallowed or spit out through the years. I remembered judging Jack Davison, the Australian carpenter, for his inefficiency in saving a pile of old bricks. Maybe it had been worth the dough it cost to hold on to them. We throw stuff away too easily in this country, and that can affect how we feel about people.

I began to accept the fact that I wasn't going to have everything and to savor what I did have. As I let go of hope (that Carolyn would want me back), I was able to let go of despair, and what I experienced then, to my astonishment, was joy. I started to feel, more and more of the time, the way I'd felt on that cold, clammy morning in Limerick.

I decided to go off the booze and took the steps to make that decision stick. A friend suggested I try meditation and showed me a simple technique to relax my breathing and silence the "roof chatter" in my mind. As I learned to practice it, I found myself in touch with God inside myself, with life, with nature, with all there is. I knew then that I always had been "the happiest son of a bitch who ever lived." I just had to keep on learning to remember it.

After a while I'd be going back to Venice to confront

my Ego, but for now I was settled in Manhattan.

In December, 1982, the children had plans to fly to New York to spend Christmas at my place. On impulse, I invited Carolyn to join them. To my delight, she agreed to come. Michele flew in from Paris. Her mother decided to visit *her* mother in America. I invited them for Christmas, too. Carolyn's mother came from Pennsylvania and my father arrived from Cambridge.

I wound up having dinner with two ex-wives, two ex-mothers-in-law, my father, all four children from the various couplings and an extra kid thrown in from the second marriage of the first ex-wife.

Carolyn and Rain got along like old friends. They hit it off splendidly. Was their secret a common enemy?

The family stayed for a week. When they flew home, I stood alone in my empty apartment and looked around at the walls. Then I began to grin. I should have been miserable, but I was miseried-out. For some reason I felt happy. No. For *no* reason I felt happy. I finally understood that I didn't need a reason. The sun was out (or it was raining), spiders were spinning webs everywhere (though in New York I couldn't see them) and life was fun (and funny). I was finally learning to lighten up. I scotch-taped Robert Frost's poem on my kitchen wall: *Forgive, oh Lord, my little jokes on Thee. And I'll forgive Thy great big one on me.*

I sat down and composed a love letter.

XVI

Darling,

Do you want to know what I remember most fondly? The silly things that made us laugh until we cried.

We took the kids to an all-day rock concert in Anaheim Stadium. Alice Cooper was the headliner. The Kinks and The Tubes were on the bill. We sat for hours in the broiling sun, up in the bleachers. The field was filled with screaming teenagers. One of our kids bought an ice cream cone, his second or third, and couldn't finish it. He passed it to you.

"I can't eat it, Mom." You handed it to me.

"Pass it on," you said.

"Huh?"

"Pass it on."

I looked to my left. A young woman in a pair of overalls sat next to me. I handed her the dripping, half-eaten cone.

"Pass it on," I said.

"What?" She looked at me in bewilderment.

"Pass it on." A smile appeared on her face. She handed the cone to the young man she'd come with.

"Pass it on," she said.

We watched the cone move past twenty people. After the tenth or eleventh, it changed directions and started going down from row to row, heading toward the field. The music blared. The people in the wake of the cone cheered its passage.

The twenty-first recipient, a sailor, never looked up to see where the cone had come from. He popped it into his mouth and ate it.

I love you. Take care.
Orson

Venice, California, 1987